ESSAY—I SAY!

WRITINGS OF ALTERNATIVE POLITICAL & PHILOSOPHICAL IDEAS

I0619613

Website Directly: www.alexaligntherapies.com

Planet Saturn - In All Its Majesty

Writings of alternative political and philosophical ideas

(Sister Book to: Wholesome Is Our Precious Gender Divide)

ALEXANDER BARRIE

ARPress
ILLUMINATING IDEAS
EMPOWERING VOICES

Copyright © 2020 by Alexander Barrie.

All rights reserved. No part of this publication may be reproduced, distributed, or transmitted in any form or by any means, including photocopying, recording, or other electronic or mechanical methods, without the prior written permission of the copyright owner and the publisher, except in the case of brief quotations embodied in critical reviews and certain other noncommercial uses permitted by copyright law. For permission requests, write to the publisher, addressed "Attention: Permissions Coordinator," at the address below.

ARPress
45 Dan Road Suite 5
Canton MA 02021

Hotline: 1(888) 821-0229
Fax: 1(508) 545-7580

Ordering Information:
Quantity sales. Special discounts are available on quantity purchases by corporations, associations, and others. For details, contact the publisher at the address above.

Printed in the United States of America.

ISBN-13:	Softcover	979-8-89356-059-6
	eBook	979-8-89356-060-2

Library of Congress Control Number: 2024903470

CONTENTS

FOREWORD

The following Essays came into being as such between the years 2010 to 2019. They present ideas based on observation and personal experience, but also from moments of extraordinary inspiration and guidance that cannot be explained mundanely but only by receiving infusions from incomprehensible dimensions. The content of these dimensions are sometimes referred to as The Akashic Records. Even so, I have borrowed much from the ancient body of knowledge called in this day and age Astrology - not 'fair-ground' astrology that most people are familiar with but from the true science of it, which is built-up over many thousands of years.

The general tone of the sum total of all the Essays is somewhat sober and some might say: Grave. It is best the reader approaches each piece with a serious mind because I have purported many answers to incomprehensible life questions that beset modern societies - indeed some of these Essays require study, and need to be read many times. In common parlance, some of them are 'hard-going'. Even so, move to the next or the following cameo that should make easier reading.

For the reader, it is better to be forewarned about the many notions expressed within the following writings because many of their content meanings are totally contrary to the present-day ideas and actions that have been pushed onto and into society by the modern media and government to the point of brainwashing it - and it, society (almost Godless) seems to be unaware of what is happening to it. In other words life's true values are becoming perverted such as to cause it [society, but not all of it of course] to accept as 'cool': profanity, disrespect, hatred, guile, indolence, cheating, lying, greed and perversion within life as normal and even as badges of honour.

Alexander Barrie. January 2020 London.

Note, that there is a certain amount of repetition in the contents of a few of these Essays, but conveyed somewhat differently in each case, because the same subject happened to be re-written at different times with additional ideas; but this partial repetition allows for better comprehension of the given subject for the reader. A few of these Essays will be difficult to comprehend, then kindly move onto others more agreeable.

FAITH V. SCIENCE

Within the present curious epoch involving mankind, an age prevalent with deranged values in every department of life, rages a great and heated debate. These visceral deliberations mostly, are exchanged by the educated and the cultivated people among us.

Their arguments have to do with Faith and Science in human life and living, and the apparent difference between the content of both - a difference such that is seemingly irreconcilable, taken their applications.

It is understood that Faith involves the deep human need of the heart to feel and to experience the agony and the ecstasy and the sacredness of life and living and what may called: 'That Otherness'.

Science exists for the many, to explain intellectually, in the cold light of day, the nuts and bolts of that life and living - which is: to identify, label, codify and prove in precise detail why and how 'It All Works': It is likened to the Written Tradition (Science and craft) as opposed to the Oral Tradition (Faith and folklore).

It would be helpful if we understood that there are certain forgotten Laws which came from 'Out Of The Void' at the genesis of human-kind, to guide us Homo Sapiens through our life-struggles.

One of these Laws is The Law of The Gender-Division (Male and Female). This Law of The Gender Division explains the reason for the two major but contrary points of view that permeate 'All and Everything' in existence.

For the moment I shall concentrate on what appear to be the two extreme junction points, Faith and Science at opposite ends of a vector, an axis that joins both of these subjects, Faith and Science together. So, the junctions of Faith, and at the opposite end, that of Science are at each end tip of this calibrated line.

The Faith Junction is Masculine (seeing the bigger/holistic picture and is of right-side brain function).

The Science Junction is Feminine (astute on unravelling the detail, and is of left-side brain function). Of course, a normal man may possibly manifest both of these qualities but with natural emphasis on the Masculine attribute, and a normal woman may possibly manifest both of these qualities but with the natural emphasis on the Feminine attribute.

The Chinese say: Man sees the bigger picture, and woman, the detail. How so?

It is a Masculine attribute that conveys, carries and reveals the 'Truth', and it is a Feminine attribute to demand the 'Proof' of that notion the 'Truth' whether in subject or in object. In other words, the Feminine attribute requires the need to 'Prove' that 'Truth'.

The visible and material primary servants of Creation for the world as we know it are the Sun and the Moon. These heavenly bodies are in charge of all and everything in existence in our world. The Sun is Masculine-*Yang,* and the Moon is Feminine-*Yin.* These heavenly Lights are the symbols that present to us the Source of all knowledge, skill and puissance that manifest in life and in this world.

Symbolically and Actually the Moon (Feminine-*Yin*) amongst other things, exists to manifest these Original Sources from the Sun (Masculine-*Yang*) in myriad ways, and enables these very Sources to be witnessed, experienced and deployed in life in all their multiplicity and majesty.

Amongst other things, the Moon's work/influence is to oversee that the gifts from above (Heaven via the Sun) are realised mundanely employing the Earth's resources to manifest them materially, for the benefit of life on, and in Earth as we know it.

In truth, and returning to Faith v. Science, we may now begin to understand, that just as Male and Female are attracted to each other similar to the opposite ends of two magnets (*Yin*/negative and *Yang*/positive) holding each other so tightly that they almost cannot be pulled apart, then Faith and Science are the 'two sides to the same coin'. They are inextricably linked – one reflecting and complementing the other when harmonious.

The Religious Faiths, reveal the ethereal and the visionary aspirations for us human beings, but may be explained in a more practical way by Science, to allow mundane comprehension for us all.

Jalal ad-Din Rumi (Sufi poet and mystic 1300 Century):
"Behind every atom (Feminine) of this world hides an
infinite (Masculine) universe".

Our eminent problem is, that we take sides and adhere furiously only to one side of the Whole without noticing that the obsession to this one side only gives us 50% of the answers to life, and therefore 50% comprehension to it only. Sadly, this is true for any subject under and above and at the sides of the Sun. The 50% that we think we know has to be defective because knowledge of the other 50% is mostly absent!

We tend only to see the opposition of two points of view and not their complementariness. Indeed these seemingly opposed points of view cannot exist without each other, as with man cleaving to woman and with woman cleaving to man!

Science with its brilliant discoveries is able to calibrate most things and thereby manifest the 'proof' of a thing – this is the Feminine attribute.

Science, able to scrutinise and to see the parts of an item by examination absolute may by this very ability, unfortunately disqualify the Masculine attribute of a given item. That is, it does not perceive the more subtle manifestations of what that item is about - yet at least!

It does not see that the part it is examining is not the Whole, and as such, the purpose or point of that item in relation to other component parts, may be overlooked.

The purpose of that item, and to understand from whence it came, requires a different but subtle faculty and a specialised kind of electrical device to measure its energetic, its rarefied atmospheric effects if any.

It is the energetic effect that is disqualified by the philosophy of Science because at the present time, the science of the present day believes that these subtle diaphanous elements hinted at above cannot be measured/calibrated* and therefore have a dubious existence.

Albert Einstein: "Science without religion is lame. Religion without science is blind".

*Energy Medicine Dr. James Oschman. In fact there are devices that do measure many of these subtle energies now confirming: The Existence of an Ethereal World and therefore: Its validity. www.alexaligntherapies.com

Alexander Barrie's Book: WHOLESOME IS OUR PRECIOUS GENDER DIVIDE - ISBN eBook 978-0-9549755-3-1 may be purchased from this Website: www.alexaligntherapies.com Or directly by telephoning: 0044 (0) 7850 908924. The printed copy maybe obtain from Amazon ISBN 978-1-951343-58-3 The subject matter of: Wholesome Is Our Precious Gender Divide is the gender phenomenon of attraction and repulsion. The Book clarifies the nature of these two opposing forces of creation as they warp and woof through all life's manifestations. This Book will be of great interest to those who question life and cannot reconcile its apparent contradictions, i.e. why there are at least always two sides to a subject, Masculine and Feminine, seemingly diametrically opposed. The contents of this Book, seeks to help to neutralise these contradictions and guides the reader into appreciating the union of opposites, i.e. Male & Female attributes inherent in every subject and in every object in life.

THE SECULAR INQUISITION OF THE PRESENT ALMOST GODLESS AGE

(An indictment on the worst of humanity at the present time 2019AD plus)

Although, in many splendid ways within the 21ˢᵗ century, we all enjoy a multitude of amenities never before experienced by humanity as such and also that we rejoice in the better laws of protection under the present modern epoch. In addition, much of humanity is involved in idealistic labours that commend the hearts and minds of the many. The many whose idealistic efforts engender a cohesive but imperative force which assists stabilisation of our culture - long may it continue **except**, we the people now exist within the ethos of a world political regime almost devoid of: Wonder and Mystery; Beatitude; Sensibility and Etiquette; and worse:

The virtual absence of the deep human need to tap into that 'otherness' beyond the pedestrian and the humdrum and sterile attributes of the present almost Godless age in which we live as Societies, is wanting. This Includes the shortage of ethics in public life and abrogation of morals and decency in private and in public life.

We have allowed, in our 'state of sleep-walking', the insidious and some of the inept aspects of the Science of the present age to crawl and to penetrate into every crevice within every subject under the Sun. This odious penetration takes the form of questioning, nay interrogating, such, as to have engendered a monster of asymmetrical proportions. This odious beast is the new age of: THE SECULAR INQUISITION. That is, everything but everything has to be <u>questioned, calibrated, bottled and corked,</u> causing **spontaneity** to be the outcast and thus, to drive all normal human-beings to the point of distraction, cynicism and tedium! Even so, this way of things does have some merit......!

We are now disallowed to enjoy spontaneity and the freedoms we used to take for granted, without interference from Governments and their Agencies. These constant but growing restrictions and constrictions are all based on the 'FEAR OF GETTING IT WRONG'. We do get it wrong because within the last 40 years plus, a dearth of FAITH* - Faith derived from holy scripture and teaching, has been and is being squeezed into oblivion. The development of <u>conscience</u> and <u>ethics</u> in truth, may only be developed and cultivated through Faith and Altruism.

Secularism has failed and is failing. We only have to witness the constant barrage of the daily news of corruption, not only in high places but also, **terrible dishonesty amongst the populous.**

* Church - the word is used eclectically, meaning all religions as well as Esoteric Study Groups. * Quote repeated here: Albert Einstein: Science without religion is lame; religion without science is blind.

This includes depravity within the Church*, but it is to a lesser degree and the problem does not lie with the Institution of the Church itself, but by those mortals/incumbents who administer within it.

In this Age fraught with ridicule, contradiction, sentimentality and feebleness, we may gain an insight as to why these dis-attributes are almost commonplace if we re-adopt the Articles of Faith*.

We may then comprehend the dangers some aspects of Science, and the way these aspects of Science have wheedled their way into every department of existence, having caused secularism to be dominant in this epoch - an epoch of Inquisition and Reductionism. Secularism has to call on the present scientific ethos to give it legitimacy.

Government (itself dubious in its executive role) cannot give real trust to Individuals or Institutions. These entities (Individuals [us] and Institutions) have proven to be unreliable, indolent and sadly, devoid of scruples in their/our actions as much as 50 percentage points at any one time! Hence, the passing of law after law after law after law ad infinitum to control our behaviour and our guile, and the oftentimes dubious actions of Institutions.

As a Physician of Natural Medicine, sadly, the critical descriptions above are born out of the experiences in the field, so to speak, and also through the lessons learnt with the sufferance that life and living tend to produce. Even so, such difficult life friction is necessary for a true and strong mental and emotional human interior and a necessary deepening for us human-beings.

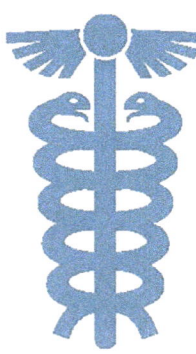

THE SUN AND MOON SUB-INFLUENCE
INHERENT WITHIN US—THE PEOPLE

There is among the populations of the world the most damaging ignorance as to the ultimate position and status and the righteousness of an Authoritative body. Authority as executed by our Monarchies, and our Heads of State. These of course are Kingships, Presidencies and Dictatorships at the focal point of the demos or the people of the land, or Tribe or Clan or Race. This absence of knowing is not necessarily the peoples' fault but is certainly the responsibility of those in powerful positions who have not informed these very peoples as to why there is at the head of their nation a single divine-right personality to which they, all of them may rally-to; but then the supporting establishment, and especially the establishment of the present day has not been educated as to the ancient reason why the execution of authority matters as revealed in the following texts.

With many nations, not yet suffering with democratic systems of government* their royal leaders are revered by their people, and in many cases also with their Presidents and even with their Dictators. It is mainly the countries with democratic governments, that have rid themselves of their monarchies. Interestingly, the very generations born within these Democratic Systems, take for granted that these present Systems of Government are the right ones and the only ones to rule a Nation. This is because they/we are Conditioned into these Democratic Systems right from the beginning of their/our lives, as we are with our religions and also as we are by the peculiar ethos of our family unit.

In the United Kingdom, it has taken near 500, some would say 1,000 years to reach a System of checks and balances, that is enjoyed today whence The Monarchy, The Government, The Military, and The Church are in balance with one another and assist the relative stability of the nation by virtue of these four great pillars of establishment as Institutions. Hundreds of thousands of people died in all the Civil Wars England suffered during this thousand year period. Yes, we are taught that there was one great and true Civil War whose protagonist was Oliver Cromwell**, but in truth there were many civil wars all contributing to the present-day relatively solid political system we all enjoy.

*It is inadvisable to think that a democracy is a governmental perfect system - it has many defects - those of us suffering the shenanigans of Brexit, in lucid moments, see the truth of democracies' foibles.

**Some say he should rest in peace and others say he should rot in hell !

These four great pillars may be thought of as representations of the Cardinal Points of the compass: East/West; North/South. This splendid arrangement that took so long to come into being, may easily be destroyed by unthinking people who have no clue as to the need of an Establishment to maintain order and stability in this unstable world in which we live and especially so within the present manic and neurotic age.

However, a democratic system of government is not necessarily the perfect one for a given nation; it depends on the character and proclivities of that people - a democratic system of government may be quite detrimental to it.

We forget that in the West our democratic system of government is not without blemish and has within it inherent peculiar deficiencies.

The Ancient Greeks considered that a democratic rulership was just one step away from actual chaos producing an unruly nation.

The esoteric law that underlies the necessity of the execution of authority over the masses, no matter what form that authority takes, is embodied within the inner meaning and the purpose/function of the Sun/Moon and the Solar System to which these Lights (Sun-Male & Moon-Female) are dominant **directing** us earthlings within The Solar System's construct.

It is not by accident that the our planets revolve around their/our central Sun. The analogy has been known since ancient times but forgotten inevitably in this, in many ways, sterile modern age. The Sun symbolises the Head of State or of Tribe or of Clan, and the Moon, its people: the Demos. However, the analogy is far greater than that which is given to the Moon in representing the Masses. Read-on:

All the planets of the Solar System play their part as servants to the Sun. Traditionally, planet Jupiter rules the diplomats, the judiciary and the ruling-classes. Planet Saturn the Law itself and The Institutions of a Country. Planet Mars the Government with executive power and the military services to back it. Planet Mercury as trade, commerce and business and Planet Venus for the social intercourse of us Beings, plus the creative arts in all its forms.

Within the Republic System, the President takes the place of the Monarch, however its government with its Prime Minister will act as executive carrying-out the necessities of rulership, though the President may have the enforcing power of a Prime Minister.

The hereditary Monarch is considered the most effective and the most absolute. This is because, just as the Sun is all powerful, stable,

and continuous so the blood line of the monarchy symbolises just that. Which is continuity as already mentioned above, and permanency just as the Sun is permanent.

The great problem for humanity is whether it's Monarch is insane or not as the case may be:

In other words, the temporary incumbent - temporary because of the limited lifetime of a given King - is healthy and wholesome and of course is sometimes not so. Hence the tendency or propensity for lesser Beings to take charge and to cast-out or murder (regicide) the King or Queen within a given historical epoch.

A further analogy essential to our Planets revolving around our Sun and which are held together and integrated by it, is of course the structure of: The Atom....with its Neutrons, Protons and Electrons.

The structure is interesting with Neutrons clustered together tightly representing the Sun and its executive power, surrounded closely by Protons acting as protectors to the Neutrons, similar to the powerful families that support and sustain the King (Neutron) and the Electrons as the people, that circle and rally-round, support and feed and nourish the central core (Sun).

A diversion at this point in thought that will be perhaps the most apposite and overwhelmingly important subject for readers to consider, but is also a little abstruse, follows now:-

We may observe that for us humans living on the earth's surface, the Sun moves over us from East to West (Northern Hemisphere) and wherever you are on this planet earth, you are subject to this solar movement in all areas of your life and living.

This is an undeniable reality and the geocentric viewpoint. Hence perhaps the justification to the existence of The Flat Earth Society that sees everything in the world and in the universe as geocentric. Also, the Sun is rising and setting every fraction of a second continuously at any given geographical place on Earth that are 180% in opposition.

From another viewpoint, in space, we see another reality that is hidden, which is planet Earth executing it trajectory, but around the Sun. This is the heliocentric viewpoint. Two realities therefore and two truths, even though you were taught at school this heliocentric viewpoint is the only truth!

The Sun, symbolically reflecting authority and leadership, may also represent analogously all those objects and subjects that may be seen, touched and experienced in the light, in this day to day world of living.

The Moon as partner to the Sun reveals for it, the Sun's unseen and hidden aspects of authority and facets of life in objects and in subjects but all within the blindness of the dark. That is: What is going-on behind the scenes and as such therefore, cannot be known, yet at least?

So we have many matters of importance, let us say matters discussed within the walls of Parliament for the people, usually laws* passed to curtail the peoples' freedoms more and more, talked about and commented upon in media news and also discussed now via social media by the people. The people mostly with their mediocre and shallow viewpoints all in the light and in the open and all this underscored and subsumed by the execution of the energetic function of The Sun. (Not that low-life newspaper - though to be fair, this newspaper may be informative and amusing!).

*The first chancellor of a united Germany circa 1870 was Otto Von Bismarck. His celebrated quote: 'Laws are like sausages, you do not want to see how they are made'.

What we do not see, or specifically, what we the people do not see, or worse, are not aware of, is what goes-on in the dark behind the scenes. This is the side of things, which are matters that carry equal and important weight but unseen if not unknown, and have just as much power, if not even more puissance as they are, in the shadows - this is the hidden Lunar/Moon aspect of creation. Analogous to the unseen dark side of the Moon.

The point being that in a Democratic System, everybody can have a say in all the matters discussed in Parliament and elsewhere, but the solutions and the opinions expressed by us, the people, and by those in authority, have to be flawed. (Read from Page 45 Noah).

This is because only half the truth of the solution has been implemented - the other 50% of the truth is unseen even denied because to manifest the true solution, the invisible 50% must be made to be revealed out of the unknown shadow world.

This would enable a perfect solution to be executed for a given problem. So when we make comments about matters with their necessary decisions, be wary, because you, we, all of us do not know the full reality, the hidden facts of any given situation. Which is one of the reasons why truth changes with every epoch and why reform after reform after reform is required virtually every ten years.

We are all too arrogant, many of us thinking we know the full answers and solutions to things at any given time - great mistake!

Further, the 'out in the open and for all to see' is Solar and Masculine. The 'veiled and concealed world' is Lunar and Feminine. This is how esoteric law views some of the psychological significances of these heavenly bodies for us humans.

Examples of decisions made and their results implemented, only to be regretted at a later date because of the unforeseen consequences from these original deliberations but still acted upon:

The most common resolve made by most of us earthlings and governed by passion, is the rushing into the love affair (Le Monde Amoureux). All is fine and dandy, until both parties get to know each other properly. It is a case of present joy over several weeks and then the relationship tainted by years of mutual torment. (One night with Venus and a life-time with Mercury! This assumes

the unhappy contraction of a venereal disease - the old way by taking Mercury for a cure). Lucky and blessed is the couple that have continuous love with and for each other on all levels over the years - such does exist. Even so, the most common saying: 'Love is Blind' is so utterly true in content. The immediate attraction and wooing activities are Solar. What will unfold in the relationship in time is Lunar - the hidden side of things yet to be revealed. Music By Alexander Barrie (have good speakers). Click-on and/or copy into your Server:
http://bandorians.co.uk/LeMondeAmoureux2.mp3

The greatest mistake, and especially so by Western Governments, was the idiotic rush to give Money, Arms, and Moral Sanction to a few psychotic hotheads rebelling within various Arab States because they wanted to be ruled under a free democratic system of government.

This is the so-called 'Arab Spring' whose springs broke causing clangors shooting-off in all directions and is still accursed to this day !

Our governments have the temerity to think that a people that has only known dictatorship since the beginning of time can do a democracy in 5 minutes! Our democratic system, still imperfect, and as stated above, has taken a thousand years to be where it is today and only just about works! (See page 14 and page 35 on Brexit).

The mentality of these people, diametrically opposed to the ethos and character of western-world culture, in truth, can only have stability politically under a dictatorship. It will take another 100 plus years, as the globe shrinks, in the sense that international relations deepen and this process widens the vista of Islamic peoples to enable them to catch-up, though in many ways our culture is 'broken'!

For the present, it is in the nature of that people, that if the 'fire-engine' or dictatorship is removed, they tear themselves to shreds. Tolerance may come to the Islamic World eventually. Even so, Looking at the bigger picture, it may be proven, in time, that Islamic attitudes and strictures were, and are, **right**, in view of universal man's appalling guile!?!?

> So, the stronger the iron fist that subjects them, the better. As the Chinese say:
> When the **tiger** leaves the mountain, the **monkeys** take charge!

That says it all !

The westernised thought that a particular non-westernised people could benefit, as we do with our kind of institutions and governmental rule, is Solar and in the open for all to see and experience and is seemingly the ideal. The reality, that was/is hidden and in the shadows is, that such a utopia is impossible to realise because in the shadows Madam Lunar dominates, and the Lunar actuality is a **dystopia** in this particular case within the Islamic world:

Islam is not only a religion, but importantly it teaches and to some extent forces onto its people a political doctrine that in so many ways is most wonderful from which The West may learn many truly great and humbling things.

Even so, Islamic doctrine is also open to misinterpretation and corruption leading to the most primitive instincts that mostly only the male gender can seemingly act-out in regard to its behaviour - behaviour that engenders intolerance and a mind-set that cannot be changed, and all made worse by the commonplace interbreeding (cousins marrying cousins; uncles marrying nieces etc.,) of some families engendering different forms of mental illness and various kinds of handicap amongst them (extreme Lunar dominance).

Islamic doctrine is oftentimes actually physically beaten into their children, mostly by their teachers! If some forethought and checking Foreign Office Archive Records going back to the nineteenth century were read and digested, all the knowledge is there to become familiar with Arab/Islamic attitudes that must preclude the slightest whiff of a democratic governmental system. In other words the authority of a ruling democratic government is **anathema** to the Islamic mode of thinking, action and being.

It seems that humanity really needs to approach every question, every topic with caution as to their resolution and because so much is unknown at any given time, humility is required throughout the process of solving the challenges that life enjoys throwing into our paths.

Parents should re-think their desires to have their sons and their daughters do in life what they, the parents, consider right and proper, when in reality their sons and their daughters are not, in so many cases, suited for such endeavours such as with the occupations the parents have planned for them. Again this is a Solar law, followed by a Lunar Law and Lunar **Rules**.

With medicine, we are offered by our doctors certain substances that help to eliminate various unpleasant symptoms from mild illnesses to severe disorders. We may even be able to continue our lives because pain and ache has been quashed. This is Solar and in the daylight, so to speak.

What is not revealed by those in charge is the eventual fallout from the actions and the hidden affects of these substances only to manifest later in life as terminal illnesses engendering an even worse physiological scenario. This is the hidden Lunar aspect. As George Ohsawa the founder of Macrobiotics said: 'What has a front, has a back'........!

Often we hear the altruist utterance that music per se brings people closer and also together, within the international scene - and seeing the bigger picture: this is a self-evident truth. The reality is different. Many musicians classically trained have a loathing for popular raucous music like Heavy Metal and other strange sounding named music - music which some might call: industrial noise !

What is generally not realised is that those with the gift of Perfect Pitch - Absolute Hearing as it is called in European Music Academies, suffer physical discomfort with certain musical sounds both music in-tune and with music out-of-tune.

The ideal of everyone coming together to enjoy music that binds people together is Solar, whilst what might be the painful reality hearing-wise is Lunar driving people apart - two truths!

In addition, oriental music of the Near and Far East that is 50% based on what Europeans loosely call the Gipsy Music Scale, naturally renders the native peoples of these areas of the world totally unable to understand Western Classical Music - which is so un-oriental. Such music and especially European liturgical music is alien to Oriental hearing as well as to and for these people absolutely.

The Sun/Moon relationship explains beautifully the successful husband career-wise and his astute, clever and dutiful wife. It may be called: 'The power behind the throne'.

Men of substance Solar have silently hidden in the background their Lunar women, who expertly guide them by the quiet gentle giving of their common-sense advice.

The sort of picture/scenario that does not readily present itself to the male gender, does so through the female.

Brexit - the people in favour of it, and the people who disfavour it:

If only the EU as a whole understood the instinctive need to allow individual Member States to have 50% autonomy, to enable it, The EU, to enjoy the other 50% constructed of harmonious common laws and customs for all The Member States !

This would mean a perfect Solar and Lunar balance. The people of an individual State would feel that their way of life in essence is not too disturbed or too changed in character - Lunar. Then simultaneously they would enjoy the ideal unity of partnership with other States - Solar.

The Lunar aspect is largely blood related and fraternal and the Solar is the utopian view of the friendship and solidarity of nations - the bigger picture.

Move over too much to the Solar aspect, so that individual identification of member countries becomes feeble and characterless, that is, all individual member states lose their ethos which is a drastic reduction of this most important Lunar aspect of belonging to a one family nation, then you generate so called Popularism. This is the demos/people rebelling against government as has happened and is happening in the United Kingdom in recent years and to date; sufficient to change the course of Modern English and European Political History.

Immigration, such an important and controversial issue of the day:

The altruistic, philanthropic, compassionate and universal way of offering sanctuary to this phenomenon is Solar in action. The fear of change of the character and of the ethos of a native people of a given country, **with their basic needs not resolved,** and when potentially flooded by immigrants, is Lunar in thought and then acted upon.

The existing ethnic people having deep roots within a particular country have to be listened-to. Ignore these peoples' justified fears and you do so at your peril. Lessons have to be learnt, but of course they never are!

In this instance, the need of a good balance between Solar and Lunar implementations; the nation family has to be considered first, regardless of the dire situation for another group of people in detriment. It is true that: 'Charity begins at home' which rankles when this truth is overlooked for the native people of a given country, if their opinions and ways of thinking are ignored.

In reality and in many instances, there may have to be a preponderance towards the Solar way of thinking and action that is always expansive/centrifugal in nature and in other ways there may have to be a preponderance towards the Lunar way of thinking and action that is condensible/centripetal in nature - it cannot always be half and half. Circumstances may disallow the maintenance of a perfect balance between both ways of thinking and action. The geopolitical background has to be examined carefully applying historical data as well.

In this way ascertainment with the correct balance of Solar and Lunar should offer the solution - the solution to a given problem, great or small.

KEY for additional comprehension to the hypothesis above:

<u>Sun-Patriarchy</u>	<u>Moon-Matriarchy</u>
METAPHYSICS	**SCIENCE**
INSPIRATION	**FORMULATION**
ILLUMINATION	**INSTRUCTION**
REVELATION	**TRADITION**
ENERGY	**MATTER**
FORCE	**FORM**
WAVE	**PARTICLE**
THEORY	**PRACTICE**
ACTIVITY	**INERTIA**
SPIRIT/*CHI*	**BODY/BLOOD**
ORAL TRADITION	**WRITTEN TRADITION**
ACTIVATION	**MANIFESTATION**
SPIRITUAL	**TEMPORAL**
VISION/EXPANSION	**REASON/REDUCTION**
LICENCE	**DISCIPLINE**
ETERNITY	**TIME**
CREATIONISTS	**EVOLUTIONISTS**

SATURNALIA

A RECKONING, WINTER APPROACHES:

I wanted to express an opinion as regards to the present instabilities throughout the world at this juncture in time, and also to mention the many personal dysfunctions we all suffer in health and in life's rough and tumble to which we are all subject. The macrocosmic reflecting the microcosmic. In other words the dysfunctions of the world are a reflection of the personal interior perturbations we all suffer, or enjoy! Put another way, the troubles and irregularities we see and witness outside of ourselves are really the projections of the way we as individuals (humanity) behave and act and think with all the full spectrum of negativity that may possibly exist.

Entering the Winter January/February 2020 for the northern hemisphere, the darkness and the aloneness of winter time; is a period that is meant for us all to be reflective in mind and to be less active in body, if we are to be close and consonant to nature's changing season. Energy consolidation and accumulation during winter time is essential if we are to enjoy good health for the remaining months of that New Year. Natural rest before activity - *yin* before *yang*.

The epicentre of the winter is relatively short; only two months long and was given in Ancient Rome to the period of Saturnalia.

This short epoch enables us to monitor the way we have been behaving towards others, and, also to face the difficult introspective task of being truthful to ourselves.

It is so necessary to question whether there is a requirement to improve our interior being, not only with one particular and important interest we may possess, but how we should be and behave in all the other subjects and issues in all the twelve great departments of life (Zodiacal Signs).

After all, what is the point of mastering a particular interest/activity, such as to earn popular recognition and increased mammon, and yet simultaneously be unaware of the necessity to improve the way we speak, the way we dress, and to be aware of our body language as well as the important need to cultivate good manners and above all, tolerance, kindness and understanding.

These very basic pointers do determine to a large extent our general health for the following new year; namely: our attitudes, strengths and weaknesses.

CLARIFYING THE TEXTS ABOVE:

Explaining further the texts above: though I mention the Roman Saturnalia Pre-Christian Era, I did not state the relevant dates and other important matters in content, and do so now:

With our present Gregorian (Pope Gregory VIII 1582) Calendar, the 60 days of darkness, contemplation and reduced activity, begins more or less around 21st December (Winter Solstice - shortest day) and continues for 60 days until 18th/19th February of the following year.

There is a certain mathematical splendour given to us in creation, and a part of that greatness is a breath-taking matrix, presented to us as the Heavenly Zodiac and its Twelve Divisions or Signs - The Zodiacal Signs that envelope the Earth. These are the **Twelve** great '**departments of life**' and each department presents a **facet** of existence - life as we know it. The twelve **facets** or **aspects** therefore, cover all possible features, items, issues, subjects and objects in existence, and in this world, and are all categorised within the **Twelve**.

Sixty days covers exactly 2 Signs of the Zodiac as each Sign of the Zodiac is traditionally given 30 equal days in length. This totals-up to the 60 days.

The relevant Zodiacal Signs associated are Capricorn for the first 30 days, and Aquarius for the second 30 days. Both these Signs of the Zodiac, one following the other, are ruled by Planet Saturn. As with all Planets (Planet from the Greek meaning: Wanderer), Saturn has a Male and a Female manifestation. The Female manifestation - **night** is given to Capricorn, and the Male manifestation - **day** is given to Aquarius. (In times modern, planet Uranus is given duel rulership of Sign Aquarius, but I will not complicate things - there are enough anomalies!).

TWO ASPECTS (of Saturn);
ASPECTS AS REFERRED TO ABOVE ARE AS FOLLOWS:

How Cosmic Capricorn works for us, is by imposing insidiously within our interior Being: caution and restraint and the recognition that success in all its forms comes with hard-work and the learning of lessons by the inevitable mistakes we make during our lifetime. Also the appreciating and the seeing of the long-view and the gaining of wisdom because of it.

This means respect for the law in all its forms - laws that assist the creation of safety, fairness and justice for all. It means also the preservation of all that is good, and it therefore rules Tradition - Tradition that brings stability to this unstable world. These attributes are the **Feminine** side of Saturn's influence whence care, safety and security are dominant. The traditional but esoteric Element is: Earth. The psychological interpretation of Earth's meaning would be: all that is mundane, stable, practical and viable. Key words: Formulation/Gravitas.

How Cosmic Aquarius works for us, is by imposing insidiously within our interior Being: the value of solidarity with the many, and the necessity of developing knowledge and skill whereby man and woman may enjoy the matters in life that have gravity, meaning, purpose, sanity and civility.

The Aquarian mode invents institutions that favour development in art, science, engineering, design, medicine and more with the dissemination of any of the intellectual gains from these subjects for the many. It means the welcoming of the new if it is of true value to the world - Invention, Creativity and Altruism means that humanity's activities do not stagnate. Ideally, spiritual development should be simultaneous with technical development?!?!?!?! Whatever, these attributes are the **Masculine** side of Saturn's influence whence intellectual curiosity, learning, and propagation of knowledge to uplift mankind's supreme status needs to be the focus.

The traditional but esoteric Element is Air - The psychological interpretation of Air's meaning would be: blue sky thinking/revelation. Key words: Inspiration/Aspiration.

It may now be perceived by the reader that planet Saturn rules amongst other things, introspection and pensiveness, but also a sense of purpose in and for all activities and erudition.

Thus, the 60 days mentioned above ideally should be occupied with deep thought, contemplation, stillness and meditation. Confidentially, monasticism and prayer is a Saturn invention.

However, because these 60 days may be such a drag to so many, and particularly for those cultures that enjoy fun and excess, especially irresponsible fun, such as with the behaviour of many of the ancient Romans, Saturnalia was established.

In this way, 60 days of partying and debauchery to enable the getting-through of that most difficult dark and cold time of the year could be enjoyed most satisfactorily.

This worst and most difficult two month time period, considered as such by many individuals, states and nations of that time, and perhaps of the present age, was/is to muddle through without suffering too much depression in the darkness of the cold winter by instituting fun and games, sex, drugs and sausage-rolls on this 60 day trial of guilt and introspection, but then, in modern-times it calculates from 60 up to 365 days of profligacy, lunacy, dissoluteness, licentiousness, recklessness, godlessness and **prozac** as normal - for many of us!

In medicine, words such as: Crepitus (a Saturnian word) from which we derive the word: Decrepit, is deployed without much thought to this word's origin.

This word describes perfectly the deterioration of a bony joint that makes a grating sound when in articulation/action. Crepitus is the name given to that grating sound of deterioration of that bony joint.

Saturn being the Lord of the Planets is also described by the Ancients, quite rightly, as Father Time. The natural acceleration and deterioration in the process of ageing that none of us may escape, is ruled by Planet Saturn. This is why the ancient Greeks considered that the greatest gift to a man was his or her premature death just before reaching old-age.

Thus, could be avoided the indignity and the decrepitude and the helplessness of this last remaining epoch of a human lifetime.

It is interesting that musically speaking in Gustav Holst's - The Planet Suite, very rarely is the superb and sublime music that describes Planet Saturn is ever played. People do not realise what they are missing with this beautiful piece of music composed by the genius of Gustav Holst.

Throughout the piece the beat of time is emphasised most wonderfully and subtly with a profound sense of resignation as to the end of life that is revealed towards and at the close of the piece.

Radio Classic FM never plays it and perhaps could never explain it, and as Noel Coward sang in his: Mad Dogs & Englishmen; 'the most brutal Burmese bandit could never understand it'!

Of course, you may try what the 120 year old man would do each day to avoid the Angel of Death's (Saturn) sweeping scythe. Because he ate a pound and a half of raw garlic every day, he was able to skip the calling. When the Angel of Death entered the old man's bedroom at midnight and tapped his shoulder as he lay in his bed, he would turn his head around to breath at the Angel profusely; saying to it as he pushed his foul breath out: "and who are you hoo hoo..........."!

Further, what is generally not recognised by the medical profession both Orthodox and Alternative, is that CREPITUS need not be a normal feature of bony joint deterioration with most of us, regardless of what the doctor says! He/she is blissfully unaware that if our pelvises could be stabilised - most of them, pelvises that is, they being dislocated in varying degrees and that includes the pelvis of the reader reading this, then most of us would not suffer pain, arthritis and degenerating bony joints - all that can be happily avoided easily.

For further understanding of this pelvic conundrum read:
www.alexaligntherapies.com

WHY DOES GOD NOT INTERVENE?

Catastrophic events both personal and impersonal may cause us to suffer a slew of unhappy and disruptive episodes in our lives the adverse consequences of which may last for many years.

As an example of personal catastrophic events in a given life may be when dramatic phenomena occur, such, as may result from a change of emotional feelings towards a spouse, for whatever reason, causing a marital chasm and subsequently a divorce. An example of an impersonal catastrophic event may be the dreaded experiencing of say, a flood that badly damages the train station which is used daily by a close family member and prohibits his attendance over several days to his workplace adversely affecting his livelihood.

There are so many examples of dramatic life incidents engendering human misery, that bring to our minds the question as to whether there is a compassionate God existing, as we are led to believe, to intervene and even to halt the destruction caused by such catastrophes by whatever means. This, both in the personal and in the impersonal within human life experience.

If life were perfect, for instance no more human travail or suffering, would that also include animals and insects, half of which are predatory, ceasing to exist because they are disallowed to feed on their quarries because pain and death threaten their victims, or something alters the predators' behaviour so they discontinue to hunt for their sustenance – do they die from starvation or do they become vegetarian in their eating habits?

We would no doubt lose half the predatory species because of the nature of their digestive systems, as these physiological systems would not or could not adapt to vegetal absorption, and so many of the predatory species would die-out, mostly by starvation.

This would mean, following the demise of many live species, an ecological disaster 'in the making', because the present biological balance, and within the so called 'food-chain' we would be presented with terrible disruption - disruption such as with the visitation of plagues of varying kinds.

Plagues of insects for example, because many of the insects would not have been consumed in the usual way (see below). As regards to the slaughtering of animals for human consumption, their unhealthy propagation, taking-up space and land, including animal food resources, must have dire consequences for the planet on which we live, and in particular, for us humans. With all the methane produced by all animals that includes us humans, contributes to Global Warming.

Take the predatory bird species for example. If they die-out, inevitably a horrible plague of flies is bound to be the consequence of this unnatural event. This is just one example of an imbalance caused by interference with the natural order of things.

Curiously, animals and insects possess a powerful sixth-sense (though not all) in that they tend to leave an area of land because somehow they know that if they stay within that particular tract of the land, they will be damaged or killed in some dynamic, disruptive and fatal event – so many animals and insects intuitively knew beforehand about the terrible impending disaster, in this case the Tsunami that took place in the Far-East some years ago, and these species left for higher ground even days earlier.

We Human-beings also have this sixth-sense, but less acutely, and therefore we do not adhere always to existential warnings.

Those human-beings who are spiritually developed have this higher sense of knowing, and subsequently may be aware of the consequences of future events – it is a feature of their spiritual progress.

Other beings, ordinary or not, do have random presentiments, but these presentiments may be misconstrued and therefore unreliable and unpredictable in manifestation and therefore they cannot be particularly useful in warning others to protect themselves. This is because of what some might call possible fanciful events that might be the product of out-of-balance imaginings!

IF LIFE WERE PERFECT, MAN WOULD HAVE TO INVENT PROBLEMS!

Returning to the natural order of things with us humans, it was
P.D. Ouspensky who gave us the statement above (paraphrased):
"If life were perfect, man would have to invent problems" ?!?!

What he meant was that man as he is, has immense potential in that he may choose whether to develop his interior 'Being' or stay as he is with his existing mental/emotional/mundane behaviour? A truly mature, that is a 'redeemed' human-being does not blame God for all and sundry when he/she is suffering adversity.

Psychologically, if he [man] stays as he is within the confines of his inner psychological, mental and emotional life, being affected harmfully or favourably by any event that occurs from his inner or outer life, should be likened to that of a cork bobbing in all directions on the waves of the sea, and at the mercy of the conditions of the sea. Such, is an excellent metaphor explaining our weaknesses as humans – we lose our anchoring so easily; buffeted this way and buffeted that way.

This is the way of things for most of us, and it also describes the interior character of our way of thinking and feeling. It portrays the present condition most of us are experiencing, and the way we conduct our lives: we tend to blame everything and everyone but ourselves when things go badly and disaster manifests!

If life were perfect, or near perfect (and the perception of what is perfect has to vary from person to person because it is a question of relativity), would we as human-beings be able to develop the various strengths required to parry successfully the different challenges that face us day-in day-out?

In terms of numbers in any engaging situation and in any challenging event, there could be say, 12 different approaches or 12 different solutions to the ramifications of that event or situation. Each person that is involved in this circumstance, with a solution or with an approach, has his/ her particular idea as to which solution and approach would work in resolving the consequent vexations engendered by this event or situation.

Similar to the metaphor of the Tower of Babel, in that it would happen that not only confusion would be witnessed amongst us because we all speak different languages, similarly because we all have different opinions, friction and uncomfortable feelings between everybody involved would be the result.

Thus, this typical kind of opposition so commonplace, and with mostly irreconcilable attitudes amongst us, would inevitably bring about argumentation.

If argumentation is the result of different opinions coming together and therefore vigorous clashing of ideas is generated, it is not difficult to consider how this sort of conflict may develop into an assault, and, an assault giving rise to open hostility, and, open hostility sparking a War between the antagonists; a War that could become international; a War that leads to many lives lost and so forth.......what has all this got do with God interceding to halt this bitter aggression becoming uncontrollable? We Human-Beings or 'Worriers' instead of Warriors as some might say, have generated this everyday and commonplace delinquency upon ourselves..................?

From the complexities of this argumentation outlined above, The Ancient Greeks (Greek Myths. Myths so called: what arrogance we moderns have!), would teach us about the effects of the actions of the numerous gods conducting the lives of all human-beings from the Heavens, as regards to their [humans] behaviour and their activities on earth. Metaphysical knowledge of other civilisations would demonstrate almost the same concepts.

THE GODS

Even the gods [planets] argue amongst themselves, and these arguments manifest within humanity, because, according to the ancients, human activity reflects heavenly occurrence. If scientific explanations are proffered then these would be about the angular relationships the planets make to one another in the heavens engendering the tensions needed to affect us humans on earth electro-magnetically and also by other means not fully understood. These other means as to how the planets affect us, are so intimately close to us, that we are blind to their presence! The Planets effects are inside us, indeed, The Planets are inside us !

Therefore all of us without exception suffer and experience the trials of the contents of: 'The Seven Deadly Sins', though the wisest amongst us might say there are more than Seven! (See Page 113).

As regards to the vexed question or conundrum as to why there are external catastrophic events, such as **earthquakes** *that appear to destroy innocent lives, and/or the unhappy circumstance of being a victim of a fateful event, because an unfortunate individual happens to be in a certain place at the wrong time, such as with a bombing perpetrated by terrorists in a civilian setting, begs the question as to God's intention, or whereabouts, or whether He is asleep or sometimes asleep as Pope Benedict pronounced following his unprecedented resignation from the Vatican Office:*

(I was told many years ago the telephone number of the Vatican. It is, or was: VAT69 !)

Confidentially: One American scientist has observed that most earthquakes happen around New and Full Moons - foolishly disputed by many of his fellow scientists!

We have to divide the deliberations to this eternal question, given above, into two parts to arrive, perhaps, at a reasonable explanation:

1. Commonplace amongst the peoples of the world, it is said, almost without exception, that those individuals suffering the effects of a catastrophe and yet appearing in the present incarnation to be innocent of any kind of guilt; guilt inviting that catastrophe as retribution administered by The Powers That Be, in a different reality may not appear actually to be so innocent, when past episodes of misdeeds executed by them in previous incarnations are taken into consideration.

They may now be redeeming these pre-historical sins by suffering the effects of these present devastating events. These past-life misdeeds nowadays, may seem to us unimportant in the scheme of things and under examination: **unscientific!**

Even so, all these happenings are relative, because certain types of events we consider in the Western World as misdemeanours for instance, are profoundly sinful in other cultures – who is to say that way of thinking is ridiculous or bad, within these other cultures? Our own Western Culture mores changes from age to age – even within one lifetime:

The ethos of our culture at any one time often becomes diametrically opposite to that which existed beforehand. Compare our attitudes in the 1950's with our sentiments in the 2000's! Within Old Testament biblical terms, it is stated (paraphrased): that the dreadful payment for the sins of the father are carried through unto his third or fourth generation.

This means that human misery and suffering of every blood generation up to the forth will be experienced by the sons and the daughters of each of these generations. Presumably this also means the sins of the mother as well, are to be suffered by latter generations?

2. For those who are truly innocent, and have been exemplary in behaviour and have carried-out good deeds, and have behaved in this splendid way within all their incarnations, and who still suffer purgatory of some kind, because they happen to be implicated in a fateful event of the present day, through circumstances beyond their control, and perhaps die as a consequence, the Cabalists argue that their "souls are needed elsewhere by God, in another time in another place" ?!?

This is an interesting statement and thought provoking, and taking in all that has just been written, goes against all the Scientific Ethos of the present almost Godless Age (A.D. 2019 plus)!

Even so, disregarding this Cabalist explanation for the moment, why will many innocents suffer, even to the point of dying as stated, or at least, their lives blighted so that they cannot in this incarnation enjoy absolute fulfilment..........fulfilment in this way redeeming their present incarnations here on Earth?

Just as the solitary chick-pea jumps out of the caldron to avoid the pain of being cooked, and is clonked back into the boiling gruel by the cook's ladle, so we as humans need to suffer a similar fate – the reason:

The cooking process with the chick-pea is there to assist the release of its goodness. It is the only way for a chick-pea, and thus, in truth, it is the only but similar process for us humans to experience and enjoy with this kind of sacred development.

We have to suffer the 'slings and arrows of the outrageous' madnesses of life to attain the true human attributes with humility, knowledge and wisdom.

Though there are times when we may be overwhelmed by the cruelty of life, as life may be so very cruel, and as such, this kind of suffering has been written about in many an illustrious tome.

HAMMER BLOWS

In music: Gustav Mahler's 6th Symphony; in the last movement we hear three neatly spaced-out hammer-blows within the symphonic musical structure. The first hammer-blow represents an event that knocks us to the floor.

We stagger about a bit in trying to stand-up again, and as we do eventually stand erect in the process of recovering from this first hammer-blow, and, we are brushing ourselves down to clean away the detritus we picked-up from the floor, and before we are fully recovered, another hammer-blow in the form of a second attack, knocks us flat-out.

It takes time now for us to recover from this second harmful event and we manage with great effort to maintain our dignity and we do everything we can to regain our original strength. This regaining of our strength is just about managed though we are weak still and the mechanics of our daily lives are still disrupted. Then unexpectedly another hammer-blow is sustained only this third one is fateful. We do not recover and a slow or if we are fortunate a speedy death ensues.

This is life, for some of us, but not for all of us: 'There by the grace of God go I'.

By God's Grace, some would say, if we survive but are handicapped in some way by this undesirable experience, we learn to do our best in the circumstances within the new limiting parameters imposed on us whether deserved or not.

Further to the discussion (Cabala) of those of us who are indeed innocent throughout their lives and are devoid of guile, we could argue as do many Hindus, that we are not so innocent as we may think, as with most of humanity, we eat meat and fish and the accumulated 'karma' over tens of thousands of years by us humans in the cruel way we kill God's creatures, determines the fate of human existence and the kismet of individuals.

Of course the quantity of 'karma' engendered per person may in some mysterious way determine his/her fate, and the kind of suffering that will occur for her/him.

In India, there are the Fakirs, probably now, a dying breed, who gladly suffer constant pain, partly to help them remember continually God's name and His mercy or wrath, and partly to redeem their accumulated sins (Karma).

Redeeming these sins repeatedly against the perpetual pain suffered via their particular method that creates this very suffering. One unusual practice, if it can be called that, is to maintain an arm above the head never lowering it, and allowing the nails of the fingers of the hand of that arm to grow, so that they curve uncut, and turn-in on themselves, and whose tips penetrate into the very flesh of those very fingers/hands accordingly!?!

There are a number of traditions, traditions of some peoples of the world, that consider the ritual slaughter of certain chosen animals, to be justified because the killing and the eating of these animals assists these animals' souls to evolve such as to occupy new-born human-beings in the processes of re-incarnation. The killing of these animals is prescribed, and has to be carried-out in a ritualised manner, with blessings for example, and is formulated to enable this kind of re-incarnation to take place. Who can argue that this is not the way to kill certain chosen animals? Even so, it is still killing and therefore it probably accumulates additional 'karma'.

This slaughter method that assists the evolution of particular animals has credibility and could be difficult to argue against. The idea that lies behind and drives ritual slaughter may indeed have merit.

So, we are supplicating God to intercede on our behalf to quash or to lessen the inevitable adverse episodes of life as they challenge us, even though we may actually deserve the punishment we are experiencing, possibly to the point where these penalisations may kill us.

Following the reading of this Essay many of us will think twice or thrice about involving God in what to many of us seem unfair cruelties to so many human-beings including ourselves at different times and what appear to be random happenings?

This whole mysterious matter may now be seen as more spectacularly complicated than originally thought because, even our going-out and our coming-in walk-wise must inadvertently kill insects we tread-on. Driving automobiles causes death to flying insects as they hit our windscreens.

When we construct buildings, we kill earth worms and so much else - the point being that we all cause suffering to living things, even though we consider this lower-order of lives not terribly important. Well, perhaps they are important in the scheme of things.

We as humans, at the pinnacle of the pyramid of creation, and given a privileged position within this magnificent masterpiece of life, should rejoice in our given status to Husband Creation - to tend to all that is angularly beneath us.

Because we are expected to respect the ramifications of all that is animate and indeed inanimate within this gigantic unit of splendour, we should, perhaps, not lay the blame at the feet of the Creator when things seem not to be right, but aspire to understand creation's deeper purpose and reason for Its/His/ Her existence, in the especial way it is ordained within the cosmos.

ALCOHOL

A NON-ORTHODOX VIEWPOINT

It is generally not realised that quaffing wines, spirits and beers should be reserved for special occasions, so too the smoking of narcotic substances including tobacco.

The Greeks arguably invented 'drinking' and even they mixed their wines with mountain water! Over the centuries and in the Western World, we have forgotten to dilute our alcoholic beverages and it has become normal to imbibe them 'neatly'. This is dangerous, because the behaviour generated by such modes of drinking cause elements within our society to become violent, deranged, accident-prone, stupor and torpor induced and detrimentally much more.

Altogether, it is costing our Country's and other Countries' economies enormous sums of money in having to deal with family disintegration and crime; criminal activities and misdemeanours which these foul habits when in extreme, tend to engender. This is because of the consequences of excess drinking and ingesting narcotics and the devastating effects these destructive habits have to the organs of the body, and especially so to the liver.

There was an Age when it was understood that the meaning and the purpose for humans to consume narcotics and to imbibe alcohol, was to induce a higher state of mind and emotion at specific times of the year, and for the emergence of an answer to an important question put by the Elders of a Tribe, or of a Nation.

In addition to the medicinal proclivities of certain narcotics, they were usually smoked by the Chiefs of a Tribe or Nation or by the Priests of that Tribe or Nation, to bring forth an important solution to a challenge that had presented itself that may have much bearing on the fate of that people – it was of paramount importance to arrive at a wise and conscious decision to help direct that Tribe, that Nation to move safely-on in its destiny.

Alcohol usually in the form of wine was and is, used for High Holy days and special Festivals to bring about a higher state of mind/consciousness to perceive the more ethereal aspects of God's joyous creation – no ill-effects were ever experienced either at the time of libation or the days afterwards. The reason why this phenomenon was possible was because the imbibers (Priests/Chiefs and laymen/parishioners) were paced in their drinking and all activities were intertwined with RITUAL usually including Prayer and Incantations.

Thus, no ill-effect could manifest for all the imbibers following the Order of the Service whether religious or secular because the quaffing was/is **in context**.

Narcotics generally were deployed to switch the minds and hearts of the takers, usually Elders, to a higher more ethereal plane, to perceive 'a truth' for a particular purpose.

Again, no ill-effect was ever experienced because the taking of the narcotics was controlled and intertwined with RITUAL and chanting (Powwow). Traditional singing and dancing usually being an essential part of the Process.

Nowadays, alas, with all our knowledge and our technical skill, we abuse the taking of the aforementioned substances, and suffer the consequences, simply because we consume them 'OUT OF CONTEXT' and for the wrong reason.

The visceral Liver is the home of the Ethereal Soul. The E.S. is anchored when housed in a healthy Liver. **The E.S. is the highest most spiritual part of our 'Being'.** The Ethereal Soul is present within us sufficient to endow our lives with inspiration, aspiration and altruism we humans may muster when we are healthy.

We may, many times enjoy the gift that the Ethereal Soul bestows, and from it that is, occasional flashes of truth from another world but higher, a world of revelation, spirituality and sublimation..

A world of majestic order to which we may have momentary access – this experience has many names according to the Religious Tradition to which we belong.

It leaves a taste of having been infused with grace, rapture and bliss, and having perceived a 'Truth'. A favourable state of 'Being', induced by the natural rituals mentioned above, may engender a moment of brilliant creativity in art, in music, in fact in any sphere of life and this includes scientific breakthroughs.

It is the visceral Liver, energetically and organically, that becomes directly affected by the intake of alcohol, and the consumption of narcotics, often within minutes and an <u>injured</u> liver in this way, becomes a negative and a detrimental place for the Ethereal Soul's residence – the E.S. may wander unanchored causing part of the mind to weaken by becoming uprooted, and this may potentially generate the worst facet of our human nature to take-over and dominate our behaviour - allowing the the parts and the aspects of our reptilian/predatory old-brain to become dominant.

Some of the positive and negative effects of these attributes and debilities are revealed in the texts above, as the Ethereal Soul abandons us to madness and even evil if it is uncontrolled and unattached by excess or abuse of alcohol and the taking of narcotics (drugs), or to bliss and revelation that may change a given life for its betterment if these narcotics/alcohols are taken with gravitas and with spiritual purposes – the choice is ours!

LEST THEY FORGET

The Alarming And The Unnatural State Of The Behaviour Of Many Women Within The Present Modern Epoch Of The 21ˢᵗ Century, And Especially So In The Western/Occidental World:

Nowadays, **an awareness and a cognisance** of the beauty, of the elegance and of the grace in the way women are meant, indeed designed, to move their bodies, does not seem to be within the consciousness of the every day human-being and indeed is stridently **absent** in the minds of the many.

Readers will notice, if they look, that if they go out into the street and view dispassionately the way the average woman walks and carries herself, you will be amazed at her absence of uprightness, grace, dignity and refinement - qualities that are the birthright of female homo-sapiens. Qualities and movements that distinguish them from the deportment of the Apes!

This **diminution** of the exquisite movement of the gracious and sophisticated woman (manly-grace almost absent in the male species anyway), is made worse, when the behaviour of so many women is taken into account, as they, the women aspire to become like their male counterparts in action and in deeds; they bastardise this feminine celestial gift of modesty that has by its very nature immense power; simply by its magnificent presence, and which possesses a magical effect upon others, especially positively upon the male gender.

Again, within this existing modern epoch, there is a characteristic of a harmful ethos causing women to try to act and to be like the menfolk, thus, the deterioration of the wonderful qualities attributed to the female can only be damaged, injured and **brutalised** and so, much of the male species may only look-on with confusion and fearfulness as the natural urge to make his way in the world becomes almost futile and somewhat nebulous. The reason: if women have lost their way, then the menfolk lose their way also.

The male gender becomes unsure of its normal status on the husbanding of the womenfolk within the close family!

Sadly, women are forgetting their essential role within the family unit: that indescribable femininity that can only emanate from the normal un-blighted female.

The un-blighted female is, without effort not interested in emulating the menfolk in their ways of thinking, habits and general behaviour!

Vive la difference! Actually, women might well enjoy worldly things, and since The First World War, and in particular The Second World War within the 20th century, they have been by necessity thrust into that fearsome, competitive spirit of both the agony and the ecstasy of the men's world - that is, this world of man mostly containing the cycles of the madness of success and of failure.

Yes, women may immerse themselves into worldly things, but simultaneously let them not forget, and let them not injure their female instincts; instincts which manifest as genteel, soft and yielding. These include delightful proclivities of good conduct, pleasant manners and <u>Modesty</u>!

Just as the ascendancy of the Working Classes in the 20th century meant enjoyment of greater all round wealth for them over several decades and that is a very good thing, concomitant with that happening, sadly, was/is a lack of good manners plus a gaping void in good breeding to go hand in hand with the increase of this largesse.

Then in the same way, women should remember their true Roll in relation to their status in Nature, that should be concomitant with the competition they now feel to get-on in the world. They should be wary of the infusion and the influences from the charms of Worldly things!

It's 'a trade-off' as many thinking people would say, and they are probably right. Even so, that wonderful loving and open quality peculiar to women is now lacking somewhat - reduced such as to cause too many unhealthy similarities between men and women.

Consequently, this inability to distinguish true and obvious differences allows us to witness within the present day many confused people actually **adulating sexual abnormality** - how far we have come away from wholesomeness and plainly perceiving the Truth!

All people should remember that women only, may produce life, women only may create life. Men cannot do this.

They, the menfolk, have to make their way in the world to make their mark and perhaps leave something of value behind them for the outside world - they are physically and mentally built to do this.

Women are now encroaching onto the mens' world also, enough to cause them, the menfolk, terrible confusion and worse: the feeling of emasculation. Trouble is, so many of my gender are stupid that they cannot see the reason for their impotence in this modern world!

ALEXANDER'S HYPOTHESIS ON GENDER DIVISION IN CREATION (ONE)

For a number of years, my binary brain has wrestled with the knowledge and with the awareness that life consists of perpetual argumentation. That is: opposing points of view in virtually all and everything in existence - there being always two sides to an argument (and probably more) and both having valid lines of reasoning and facts to justify their legitimacy.

Being associated with, but also steeped-in the practice of Oriental Medicine and Philosophy has brought home to me the importance of the theories underlying the meanings and relationships between *Yin* and *Yang*; Sun and Moon; Heaven and Earth and more. I will explain:

All traditions, no matter from where they originate, all have, more or less, at their genesis: In The Beginning God Created Heaven & Earth. Or at least:

In the beginning Heaven & Earth were created. This is a statement of gender division in all that is under the Sun and beyond, in that the Masculine aspect is given to Heaven and the Feminine aspect is given to Earth by many peoples' Traditions.

What does this mean?

It means that there is a fundamental Law underlying existence for everything to come into being. This is the Law of the Masculine and the Feminine division in all that is before our eyes, ears, tastes, smells and touch senses – in all that is Manifest. Also, the same Law applies to all that may be perceived only by our 'higher senses/faculties', beyond sight, sound, odour, touch and taste, i.e. we may perceive all that is Un-manifested with our 'higher faculties' (if they are awake!).

Nevertheless, the Un-manifested may be felt and experienced at curious moments in a given life, mostly unexpected! The Un-manifested tends to be ethereal, notional, theoretical, rarefied, and somewhat more encompassing.

The Divisions below explain to some extent the curious ideas referred to above:

The Un-manifest - Heaven (Father)		The Manifest - Earth (Mother)
Metaphysics	v.	Science
Inspiration	v.	Instruction
Revelation	v.	Tradition
Illumination	v.	Formulation
Energy	v.	Matter
Force	v.	Form
Wave	v.	Particle
Activation	v.	Manifestation
Theory	v.	Practice
Activity	v.	Inertia

In life, in existence, there is a classification in all and everything divided between the Masculine and the Feminine. This means that all objects and in all subjects in creation may be classified as either Masculine or as Feminine.

Most languages have this sensibility of gender division. The English language had it once, and in my opinion is the poorer for not having this characteristic since the thirteen hundreds?!?!

Understanding this forgotten Law would help persuade us to comprehend that the seemingly opposed forces of opposition, are in reality both valid and merely two sides to the same coin, but have an inherent different basis. One view is always qualitative Male and the other view always qualitative Female.

At this juncture it is important to explain that these writings are not biased towards the Feminine attribute nor the Masculine attribute - both attributes are equal and both cannot exist without the other as is obvious in man and in woman. Man's masculinity is simply greater in him and less so in the Female. Women's Femininity is simply greater in her and less so in the Male. Both sexes have both attributes of male and of female but of different degrees, engendering that magnificent difference.

Humanity has largely forgotten this fundamental Law of Gender Division. There would be fewer disputes, arguments and wars if we could remember and live by the values of this Law, as well as comprehending its purpose in, and for Creation. Tolerance and appreciation is required by us all, allowing both gender divisions and therefore viewpoints, to flourish.

My Thesis, turned into a small tome, to some extent explains amply all that is needed for us to know and to understand how this Law acts as a thread that conjoins all of life that we see with our eyes and more, and this is the tangible, but also the life that we do not see as such, that tends to be ethereal and nebulous. (Wholesome Is Our Precious Gender Divide ISBN 978-0-9549755-3-1. Alexander Barrie available as eBook from Website: www.alexalign.com).

Further, we may perceive at special moments this side of existence that we do not readily recognise, or experience, at special moments via our interior 'higher centres or faculties' - the faculties that some scientists, unhappily deny exist – and enjoy new understandings engendering a more harmonious interior life for us all........and therefore in turn we may enjoy a more harmonious external life - the external life that we try to change without the recognition for the need essentially to change the individual **inner** life first or at least initially.

Why is it we wish to change for the better the existential life and not our inner lives at the beginning - the outer life is a reflection of our inner lives? Change our inner life with awareness and mindfulness, and a more wholesome outer life will follow naturally!

> **Albert Einstein**: The reason for Time is so that Everything does not happen at once.
> (**Time**: Feminine. **Everything** in this context: Masculine)

ALEXANDER'S HYPOTHESIS ON GENDER DIVISION IN CREATION (TWO)

(There is to be expected some repetition from # One above, but with subtle differences)

As earlier stated, for a number of years I have mentally wrestled with the need to comprehend why, as to the fact, that life has always two opposing points of view in virtually all and everything in existence - there being always two sides to an argument (and probably more), both having valid lines of reasoning and facts to justify each their legitimacy. For example the advantages and the disadvantages of Britain staying with the EU or leaving the EU (2019 A.D.). See pages 22 and 49.

Being immersed and involved within the fields of Oriental Medicine and Philosophy has brought home to me the importance of the theories underlying the meanings and relationships between *Yin* and *Yang*; Sun and Moon; Heaven and Earth etc., My hypothesis commends the reader to consider that opposing points of view in subject and in object, are either Masculine or Feminine in attribute.

That is, either a subject or an object may be classified as being either masculine or feminine in nature - therein lies the seed to opposition, or contrary point of view, but is this so? See below:

All traditions, no matter from where they originate, all have, more or less, at their genesis: In the beginning God made Heaven and Earth. Or at least: In the beginning Heaven and Earth were created. This is a statement of gender division in all that is under the Sun and above the Sun, in that Masculine is given to Heaven and Feminine is given to Earth.

What does this mean? It means surely, that there is a fundamental **Law** for everything to exist, for everything to come into being. This is the **Law of the Masculine and of the Feminine Division** in all that is before our eyes......in all that is manifest. In addition, the same **Law** applies to all that may be perceived only by our 'higher senses', beyond: sight, sound, smell, touch and taste, i.e. we may perceive all that is un-manifest with our 'higher faculties'.

Nevertheless, the un-manifested (Masculine) may be felt and experienced in curious moments in a given life, mostly unexpected! The un-manifested tends to be ethereal, notional, theoretical, sometimes what is nowadays called: 'blue sky thinking'! The un-manifested tends also to be more encompassing.

Traditionalists might draw attention to these marvels emanating directly from Heaven but present-day Science may described them as being so very centrifugal in nature, as to be too nebulous and therefore immaterial!

With material/mundane life, in objects and in subjects actually manifest, these are given to the Feminine - the scientific definition says that the action and manifestation of these is centripetal and therefore somewhat denser or tighter.

Most languages continue to divide their nouns and adjectives into Masculine and a into Feminine Form. Our English language enjoyed this gender division once, and in my opinion is a little deficient for not having this virtue since the thirteen hundreds?

It is therefore, more difficult for English Speaking Peoples' to comprehend this natural classification in all of our life's departments, partly because we neutered our language Long ago.

Understanding this forgotten Law would help conduce us to comprehend these seemingly opposed forces of opposition, when in reality both these views of opposition are legitimate and merely two sides to the same coin, but have an inherently different basis.

One view is always qualitative Male and the other view always qualitative Female - they cannot exist without each other - **the Feminine attribute giving <u>Form</u> to the Masculine attribute of <u>Theory?</u>**

*Humanity has largely forgotten this fundamental **Law of Gender Division**. There would be fewer disputes, arguments and wars if we could remember this **Law**, and comprehend its purpose.*

IT IS INTERESTING THAT WHEN THIS GENDER THEORY IS APPLIED TO BRITAIN AND TO EUROPE, THE MASCULINE POINT OF VIEW IS ACTED-OUT BY BRITAIN AND THE FEMININE POINT OF VIEW THAT OF EUROPE. THE MASCULINE ETHOS IS TO ENJOY FEWER LAWS AND THE ETHOS OF THE EU IS TO IMPOSE MORE LAWS. THE MORE LAWS THE BETTER AND THAT IS THE NATURE OF THE FEMININE ETHOS. ONE IS TOWARDS FREEDOM AND THE OTHER IS TOWARDS RESTRICTION.

THE UNDERLYING REASON BRITAIN DESIRES INDEPENDENCE IS THAT HE CONSIDERS, ACCORDING TO HIS NATURE THAT ALL HIS FREEDOMS ARE BEING AND HAVE BEEN CURTAILED - THIS HAS BECOME INTOLERABLE TO THE NATURE OF THE BRIT AND THE ALBION.

IF THE LAWS THAT WERE/ARE PASSED BY THE EU COULD BE FEWER AND LESS SUFFOCATING, THEN WE BRITISH WOULD WANT TO STAY WITHIN THE MARRIAGE. WHAT HAS HAPPENED IS THAT THE FEMININE SIDE TO RESTRICT AND TO CONSTRICT AS EXECUTED BY [IT] THE EU HAS BECOME DOMINANT, THEREBY GENERATING IN OUR EYES AN UNFAIRNESS THAT WE THE BRITISH FIND UNACCEPTABLE. OF COURSE, BALANCE IN A PARTNERSHIP MATTERS.

EVEN SO, IN MY HUMBLE OPINION WE CANNOT FULLY PROSPER BEING OUT OF THE E.U. WE HAVE FORGOTTEN THAT WE WERE DOING WELL IN TRADE & INDUSTRY AND BECOMING WEALTHIER AND STRONGER AS A NATION. OUR DAYS OF EMPIRE ARE LONG GONE AND OUR DESTINY LIES WITH EUROPE.

AGAIN WE HAVE FORGOTTEN THAT BEFORE WE JOINED THE COMMON MARKET (AS IT WAS CALLED IN THE EARLY DAYS), WE WERE KNOWN AS THE POOR AND THE SICK MAN OF EUROPE AND WE SUFFERED STRIKE AFTER STRIKE AFTER STRIKE IN INDUSTRY AND MORE. NOW WE HAVE BEEN DRAGGED INTO THE 21ST CENTURY AND THAT IS WHAT ULTIMATELY MATTERS, WE ARE BETTER PLACED THAN EVER BEFORE IN THAT IT IS TRADE AND INDUSTRY THAT MATTERS; IT PAYS THE BILLS.

HOWEVER, SINCE WE ARE A VERY, VERY INVENTIVE AND A VIGOROUS RACE, WE SHOULD USE, IN MY OPINION, OUR BRILLIANT TALENTS 100% TO BUILD A NEW KINGDOM IF WE TRULY EXIT FROM THE E.U. EVEN SO, IT MAY TAKE 20 YEARS TO RECOVER ECONOMICALLY - HAVING SHOT OURSELVES IN THE FOOT!

THE CURIOUS PRESENT DAY REQUIREMENT OF GENDER, MALE & FEMALE TO BE UNHEALTHILY SIMILAR - THUS DAMAGING OUR EXQUISITE INHERENT DIFFERENCES.

THIS IS AN HYPOTHESIS: OFFERING THE PROBABLE REASONS
WHY INSANITIES DERIVE FROM THE RESULTS OF TWO OPPOSING POINTS OF VIEW,
MASCULINE v FEMININE, WITH ANY SUBJECT UNDER, ABOVE AND AT THE SIDES OF THE
SUN. EVEN SO, LONG LIVE THE DISTINCTION AND THE DIFFERENCES BETWEEN THEM!

AND FURTHER:

This fundamental law within phenomena; and a phenomenon cannot exist without this law, is the canon of duality (male/yang and female/yin) within everything in existence whether in subject or in object:

THIS 'HYPOTHESIS' CONVEYS THE IDEA THAT THE LAW OF GENDER
DIVISION MAY BE AT THE HEART OF THE CONUNDRUM OF CONTRARINESS,
BUT GENDER DIVISION NOT QUITE AS WE KNOW IT:

Male/Yang/Heaven presents its inspired formulas left-hand column below - and in time, these formulas surrender to their material reflections as revealed in the right-hand column that is Female/Yin/Earth. The modern day conundrum manifestly is that the matters of the right-hand column have become crystallised and sacred allowing very little of the new

into their realm as they become orthodox and absolute as Traditions do - The Tail Wags The Dog - as happens in the political arena when extremes of either the far left or the far right dominate society within a particular epoch, and all the rigour that this means......

Male/Yang/Heaven (solved)	*Female/Yin/Earth (resolved)*
METAPHYSICS	SCIENCE
INSPIRATION	FORMULATION
ILLUMINATION	INSTRUCTION
REVELATION	TRADITION
ENERGY	MATTER
FORCE	FORM
WAVE	PARTICLE
THEORY	PRACTICE
ACTIVITY	INERTIA
SPIRIT/CHI	**BODY/BLOOD**
ORAL TRADITION	WRITTEN TRADITION
ACTIVATION	MANIFESTATION
SPIRITUAL	**TEMPORAL**
VISION/EXPANSION	**REASON/REDUCTION**
LICENCE	DISCIPLINE
ETERNITY	**TIME**
CREATIONISTS	EVOLUTIONISTS

"Behind every Atom [*Yin*] lies is an Infinite Universe [*Yang*]" Rumi 13th Cent. Sufi Mystic.
"The reason for **Time** [*Yin*] is so that **Everything** does not happen at once [*Yang*]" Albert Einstein.

This hypothesis should not be thought of as a competition between the male and the female - it is not a case of which gender is the better. A normal man has a percentage of the female in him, and a normal woman has a percentage of male in her. In the matters of the left-hand column (Masculine/Yang) its INTELLECT and its IDEAS cannot manifest other than through the VESSEL, STRUCTURE and STABILITY of the matters of the right-hand column (Female/Yin)! These nomenclatures for us English Speaking Peoples' may be difficult to understand as our language was neutered by design or by default under the Saxon Kings long ago and so we are insensitive to the exquisite differences in the gender values of nouns and adjectives when in English usage!

REPEATED:

WHAT APPEAR TO BE OPPOSITES ARE ACTUALLY COMPLEMENTARY AND PARTS OF A WHOLE

GENDER VALUES: THE ETHEREAL ORIGIN (HEAVEN) OR GENESIS OF ALL PHENOMENA (YANG/MASCULINE) DERIVES FROM THE ABSOLUTE OR PRIMUM MOBILE AND IN THEIR DESCENT THROUGH DIFFERENT LAYERS OF FINENESS OF MATTER - MATTER THAT BECOMES MORE DENSE AS IT REACHES THE FULLNESS OF THE TEMPORAL, THAT IS:

BECOMING FULL YIN/FEMININE (EARTH). IN THIS CONTEXT, FEMININE/YIN IN NATURE IS CENTRIPETAL IN ACTION AND MANIFESTATION - BUT A FORCE THAT IS INWARDS AND UPWARDS IN EXPRESSION. YANG/MASCULINE IN NATURE IS CENTRIFUGAL IN ACTION AND ACTIVATES AND EXPRESSES ITSELF OUTWARDS AND DOWNWARDS.

Interestingly, we now have the virtual discovery of the 'God Particle' (Higgs Boson) and, this 'God Particle' is indeed a component of the origin of Mass. That is: Ostensibly formless energy/impulse initially (masculine/yang), followed immediately by a condensation into 'Mass' and then: Structure (feminine/yin).

Consider that altogether, it is a matter of the diaphanous and the nebulous descending to denser stages of materiality and centrality.

The lighter and the more ethereal (Intellect/ideas) is indicated at the left-side column above (Masculine - Yang) and the heavier and the more dense (physical actuality), at the right-side column (Feminine - Yin).

The full Spectrum from the fineness and mercurial, to the heaviest and most condensed contains within it all possible phenomena **in different ratios** of course, depending on what degree happens to be occupied within this Spectrum of creation.

Applying the texts above to well-being, the most natural balanced state for us human-beings health-wise, in our thoughts and in our feelings, in our spiritual leanings, and in life generally, has to be in or near the centre of this - what is actually - a calibrated Spectrum. In our Bodies, and in Nature, the natural checks and balances are present to keep us as close towards the centre of this Spectrum as is possible; only then is there health and wholesomeness - our lives and our communal histories reveal to us what dangers manifest when we move away or are moved away from this centre arena towards anyone of the extreme ends of this: Our Creational Life Spectrum! A desired balanced state is when Yin & Yang are in balance, that is, they are neither too centrifugal nor too centripetal inherently.

WHY ARE WE HAVING TO ADHERE TO SET PROCEDURES DENYING SPONTANEITY?

In the present epoch there is a damaging bias towards matters of the right-side column; meaning: The suffering of internal and external derangement because of the possible **crystallisation** (living imprisonment) in, and of all things as there is almost an absence of enlightenment, consciousness and conscience - attributes of the left-side column!

In the World and in the Western World in particular, since the advent of and expansion of <u>certain aspects</u> of Science, we have indeed become obsessed by Reductionism that has been given immense importance (Feminine right-hand column). In our way of thinking and in our use of language, we have become mechanical when expressing ourselves - form and structure has lulled us into a kind of somnolence. There is safety in structure and routine - but only an awareness of our greater spatial universe and that

which derives from 'out of the void' (Masculine left-hand column) may help balance our consciousness, to enable equality between the mechanics of mundane life (Feminine - right column) and the wakefulness of metaphysics (Masculine - left column)!

The right-hand column's subjects are the ones whose meanings and applications have sadly become dominant in this detrimental epoch, that is, in the present historical ethos in which we mankind are subject, but especially so, in the Occidental/Western World. See additional material: Noah Today page 61!

All the mundane formulae within the subjects in the right-hand column (Feminine/Yin) are the ones that really matter to us nowadays. They matter so much that we have forgotten from whence they originated. The genesis of these are indicated in the left-hand column (Masculine/Yang).

Today alas! we must calibrate and write-down and record label and bottle everything, for fear of loss, and because of criminal and dishonest behaviour, but also from 'losing face' because we cannot trust ourselves and others.

In this sad state-of-affairs, with our advances in technology, know-how and cleverness! Most of us are as primitive as ever in our emotional and psychological responses as well as being unable to perceive the 'bigger picture'.

WE LIVE IN AN ALMOST GODLESS AGE AND LITTLE IS VIEWED AS SACRED

Because of this, in our present almost **Godless Age**, we use aspects of Science (right-side column) more and more to explain all phenomena and indeed, we use features of science to moralise and to guide us - and all this, to fill the vacuum left by the demise of the Church of the present day, or at least because of the waning influence of it (left-side column).

The Church* used to assist and to guide us ethically through this very difficult life; a life that is full of temptations to rouse the passions. These temptations are perfectly normal and acceptable when as desires they are in balance, in their proper place, and wholesome, and guided by moral fortitude - qualities which our religions are meant to instil in us or, obtained and understood via spiritual practices not necessarily belonging to any particular religion (column left).

*Used eclectically meaning all religious institutions.
Albert Einstein 1879-1955: "Science without religion is lame, religion without science is blind."

In these modern times we mistakenly think we are moral and just, but as governments pass law after law after law after law to regulate us more and more by the hour, with the setting-up of Quango after Commission after Committee, Reformation after Reforming after Reform, it may now be perceived by us, in a lucid moment (if we are lucky to have a lucid moment) that this perverted way of doing things is mostly and blatantly barely working (subjects of the column right above).

Secularism is trying to take the place of the 'grace and humility' that may only come from the 'Fear of God' or the profound recognition that there is something out there, or up there, or better: **within us,** that is sacred and infinitely powerful, and that we go, in reality, "There by the grace of God." The word 'God' is used here also to cover: The Absolute; The Prime-Mover; Primum Mobile. The Cogent, engendering creation etc.,

It is not working because <u>facets</u> of science/secularism provide only 50% of the answer to life, even though these scientific facets arrogantly most often think it answer 100% of life's conundrums (column right).

Also, mankind unchecked from within itself, by itself: 'Self' - i.e. being our own judges but from within, deep with our Being, our behaviour is such as to cause governments to pass more and more and more laws to restrict and to constrict us (column right).

Prince Otto von Bismarck: 1815 -1898. First Chancellor of the German Reich:
"Laws are like sausages, it is better not to see how they are made."

So, we are back where we started! Long ago when the Church (Masculine/Yang) controlled everything including our actions, and left virtually no freedom to explore life, and was too constricting when *in-extremes.*

We are now all bathed in the diametric opposite *in-extremes*, which is in the scientific and the secular. It [The Church] has given-way to this new way of things, which for us also means libertarianism, possibly at its worst. Science is The New Church!

THE SECULAR INQUISITION IN THE WESTERN WORLD PART TWO

With Some Repetition

Nowadays, we are all suffering the effects of **A Secular Inquisition** (born of the right-hand column above) led by particular standpoints of Science. Particular standpoints of Science (not the whole of the scientific mode of course) because we have made way for calibration to be carried-out in every department of life i.e. exactitude has become an absolute necessity for all 'Laws' passed, if they are to be coded/written and implemented. Laws passed such as to engender more tedium within the demos, and in truth, irksome to the very people who make these Laws!?! In time these laws that seem to be written in stone, **Change,** and at a different Age become diametrically opposite in effect, to their original intention and meaning.

Truth in one epoch become a lie in another epoch. What is perceived to be truth held at a given time by those who are implacable in their thinking and actions may experience a rude awakening when it is proven eventually that the views they held at this one time become moribund in another future time........ 'What is truth' asked Pontius Pilate!

SO, THE RELIGIOUS RESTRICTIONS ONCE IMPOSED ON US LONG AGO (born out of left-hand column) ARE NOW SUBSTITUTED BY PARTICULAR SECULAR/SCIENTIFIC RESTRICTIONS (Born out of right-hand column) BECAUSE WE HAVE PROVED AS HUMANS NOT TO BE WORTHY OF LIVING A LIFE THAT IS WHOLESOME AND WITHOUT ARTFULNESS!

The cogent argument of this Essay is to bring observance to the law of creation. A law that is common to all traditions and that issue from most ancient cultures and which state:

THAT WHICH CAME OUT OF THE VOID AND WAS CONCEPTUAL WAS FROM THE MASCULINE ASPECT OF CREATION (Left-side column. Right-side of brain manifestation).

THAT WHICH WAS TANGIBLE, MATERIAL, VISIBLE AND FUNCTIONAL, WAS FROM THE FEMININE ASPECT OF CREATION (Right-side column. Left-side of brain).

FOR AN IDEA TO MATERIALISE IT HAS TO PASS FROM BEING ABSTRACT TO BECOMING CONCRETE. THAT IS FROM MASCULINE/YANG TO FEMININE/YIN.

AN ABSTRACT CONCEPT CAN BE THOUGHT OF AS A 'TRUTH' (Solar) BUT THE CONCRETE MANIFESTATION CAN BE THOUGHT OF AS THE 'PROVING OF THAT TRUTH' (Luna).

The Feminine attribute, amongst other things, is a requirement to 'prove the truth'. Proof is a Feminine attribute and is hinted at in the right-side column above.

As already stated, in this present epoch we are solely obsessed with the matters indicated at this right-side column. We have forgotten the attributes of the matters at the left-side column:

*1. Of the left-hand column, the genesis of the Yang/Masculine aspect of the ramifications of a subject or of an object tend to be conceptual and therefore Revelation, Inspiration, Illumination, Transcendence, Theory, and the wisdom of the ages (interior and exterior wisdom) brings into being, knowledge of the 'bigger picture' without the employment of scientific laboratories to **'prove'** the nature of the subject under examination. This is because the Masculine is linked to Heaven, Force, Metaphysics, 'Energetics', Sun and 'Yang' and in essence represents, and from which issue, the **original plans** of **'all & everything'**, and is also surely a purveyor of a valid viewpoint and whose subjects may all be implemented and have all to do with POSSIBILITIES.*

2. Of the right-hand column, the genesis of the Yin/Female aspect naturally demands proof or evidence of the ramifications of a subject or of an object. The nature of these demands are in the form of Calibration, Examination, and for its parts to be notated and listed, proven and more. This is because Formulation, Discipline, Tradition, Science, Matter, and Moon looks to the mundane and the practical, and is also a perfectly valid viewpoint and whose subjects may all be implemented and have all to do with Everything that is Actual, Temporal and Definite.

The threads (Male and Female) that conjoin all and everything in concert in every object and in every subject, are bound collectively (Male and Female) in all that is manifest in this world, and are in pairs; one part Masculine - Yang (left-hand column) and one part Feminine - Yin (right-hand column).

This **Law** of two Forces, Male and Female are inextricably linked, as they are, in the animation of the DNA chain, and as they are in Wave (Masculine) and in Particle (Feminine). Nothing can come into being without the interplay, warp & woof of these two gender aspects - these two Forces.

Most of us are unable to be objective, for whatever reason, sufficient to enable the essential perceiving of two seemingly opposed points of view, Masculine and Feminine as being two parts of a whole, and therefore complementary.

THE TOPIC OF ALTERNATIVE MEDICINE VERSUS ORTHODOX MEDICINE FOR EXAMPLE MAY EXPLAIN BETTER THE ARGUMENTS PUT FORWARD ABOVE:

ORTHODOX SCIENTIFIC MEDICINE

Trauma aside, which is usually dealt with admirably by scientifically based **orthodox medicine,** orthodox medicine's ethos is such as to require experimentation with chemical substances, usually to allay or quash pathological symptoms presented by the patient, but also the cutting-out, or the cutting-off, of the offending part that belongs to that patient - that body part that happens to be bad, offensive, ailing and just a plain nuisance! Experimentation is usually performed in the scientific laboratory. Its aim is to find a way to eliminate an illness, post-haste, but also to name and notate it and to find a substance to cure it. In reality, it is a substance that will merely help to eliminate the symptoms of a pathological condition - thus, the allopathic (right-hand column) approach.

A cure does not necessarily come into the equation, if it does, it is probably by default, unless infection is the problem and especially infection originating from tropical countries; and this would be dealt with admirably by orthodox medicine, though not always!

By understanding the **keys** given above, it will be perceived by the reader that **Orthodox Medicine** is a **Feminine** facet to the practice of medicine, requiring absolute diagnosis of the ailment in question and the detailed way in which it is to be eliminated.

TIMELESS INTUITIVE ALTERNATIVE MEDICINE

With **Alternative Medicine,** its ethos is diametrically opposite to that of orthodox medicine as the 'bigger picture' is taken into consideration when accessing the pathological model the patient presents.

The requirement is to question life-style and habits of the patient; his/her energetic presentation, i.e. body-language and the perceptions of the practitioner as to the patient's overall aura or light (Chi) or non-light as the case may be, emanating or not emanating from them.

In addition, what are the events in their lives at the present time affecting their body/mind/**emotions**/spirit!

Most of us, therapist or no, may intuit the condition of a patient by this exudation or non-exudation of light and energy, which says so much to the therapist. The therapist may now make deductions as to how treatment should be applied and as to the type of treatment plan to be engaged.

Treatment models are mainly connected with the need to bring an energetic balance back into the soma.

The philosophy underlying alternative medicine embodies the realisation that most pathological conditions are due to electrical and biological (energetic-chi) stagnation in a given area or areas of the body.

Morbidity arises, whether mental emotional or physical from this out-of-balance state. The methods of resolving these dysfunctional parts, these morbid accumulations, in the visceral and in the other bodily tissues applied in alternative medicine, are usually in the form of some kind of body-work and possibly the administering of herbal substances - substances that generally do not damage other bodily tissues with their chemical actions.

There are, of course, more specific ways of diagnosing a pathological disorder by the therapist employing alternative medical means (mostly ways which are born out of oriental-medicine), but the way described above is one that dares not speak its name in the current scientific obsession to measure all and everything to exactitude and to the point where many of us are driven to distraction and boredom.

Actually, the spiritual and the higher cultivated centres in us all, whether awakened or not, do determine to a large extent the kind of pathologies, if any, that will manifest during our life's development.

These, so important, are not taken into consideration by Orthodox Medicine. I recommend to the reader to Read: **Anita Moorjani - Dying To Be Me.**

By understanding the **keys** given above, it will be perceived by the reader that **Alternative Medicine** is a **Masculine** aspect to the practice of medicine, requiring a universal appraisal to the ailment in question and the taking into consideration of the long term effects of its treatment models and applying a wider and a more all-encompassing contact.

DEPENDING ON THE TYPE OF DISORDER THE PATIENT SUFFERS, BOTH ALTERNATIVE AND ORTHODOX MEDICINE HAVE THEIR PLACES, AND IN PERHAPS 50% OF INSTANCES AN ORTHODOX APPROACH IS BEST, AND IN THE OTHER 50% OF INSTANCES PERHAPS ALTERNATIVE MEDICINE MAY BE THE BETTER APPROACH TO EMPLOY ALTOGETHER, MEANING LEGITIMACY OF, AND ACCEPTING THE TWO SIDES TO THIS ISSUE WITHOUT BIAS, THIS ECLECTIC METHODOLOGY.

NB:

Again: It is probable that for us English Speaking People, the concepts of the Masculine and the Feminine divisions in phenomena are difficult to countenance, and this is no doubt partly due to one main <u>impoverishment</u> in our splendid language.

Our language, that is now paradoxically universal, <u>was neutered in its nouns and adjectives usage under the Saxon Kings</u> by accident or by design, almost a thousand years ago - because of this, and opposed to other languages, we have become <u>insensitive</u> to the subtle nuances of male and female nomenclature within all phenomena, in my opinion!?!?

NOTE: Two Aspects of Erudition:

1.

Take a given body of knowledge such as Geography. For such a compilation of knowledge to come into being, the human faculty of curiosity had to be present with a mathematical bent to identify, name and to calibrate all areas of land mass and topography - this body of knowledge did not require 'revelation' or 'illumination', just an abstract inspiration initially (Masculine) to capture and to dominate the land, usually for practical purposes (Feminine).

2.

Take a compilation of knowledge such as with the Bible or any other great inspired works including the Genius of Scientific Invention, and Creation within the Arts.

For such knowledge to come into being, revelation, illumination and vision from out of the ether (but actually from deep within) was the initial impulse (Masculine), before the development of the Traditions that came into being (Feminine) as demanded by 'Revelation' - indeed commanded by 'Revelation', to enable itself to have 'Form' and therefore identity by the application of skill.

This distinction between number 1 and number 2 above should indicate that number 2 in comparison with number 1 has an ethereal celestial genesis whilst number 1 has a genesis but from the human mind by which is formed the conception of an idea - yet both still have an abstract beginning and therefore Masculine in nomenclature!

Returning to the original theme within the captions of this Essay (above), namely the contrariness that exists within every subject in existence, of which two seemingly contrary and intractable points of view arise, these may now be understood as either a Feminine or as a Masculine division, the Masculine being the more abstract and ethereal, and the Feminine as being the more tangible and practical. Both in reality being two sides to the same coin.

NOAH TODAY: Below is an email probably sent around the world but without an author's name to it. I have cleaned it up a bit to make it more presentable - I'm sure whoever the author is, will not mind the piece being published. Its meaning, though with humour, is of the utmost importance and in a way supplies the essence of what the Essay above on Gender Divide is all about - the madness and complications of rules and regulations gone berserk! (right-hand column in the essay above) because of the absence of the wider consciousness of 'The Bigger Picture' (left-hand column in the essay above). Also, importantly, it indicates quite clearly the defects of a Democratic System of Government, where anybody can have his/her say and nothing substantial gets done as originally conceived! Those of us living under the Brexit debacle will tragically confirm this!

Enjoy:

NOAH TODAY: In the year 2020, the Lord came unto Noah, who was now living in England and said:

"Once again, the Earth has become wicked and over-populated, and I see the end of all flesh before me."

"Build another Ark and save two of every living thing along with a few good humans." He gave Noah the blueprints, saying:

"You have 6 months to build The Ark before I will start the **unending rain for 40 days and for 40 nights**" !?!?

Six months later, the Lord looked down and saw Noah in his yard weeping - and no Ark. "Noah!" He roared, "I'm about to start the rain! Where is the Ark?"

"Forgive me, Lord, begged Noah, but things have changed for the worse under the System we are governed by":

"I needed a Building Permit. I've been arguing with the Boat Inspector about the need for a Sprinkler System."

"My neighbours claim that I've violated the neighbourhood By-Laws by building the Ark in my back-garden and exceeding the height limitations. We had to go to the Local Planning Committee for a decision."

"Then the Local Council and the Electricity Company demanded a barrel load of money for the future costs of moving power lines and other overhead obstructions, to clear the passage for the Ark's move to the Sea. I told them that the Sea would be coming to us, but they would hear none of it."

"Getting the wood was another problem. There's a ban on cutting local trees in order to save the Greater Spotted Barn Owl. I tried to convince the environmentalists that I needed the wood to save the Owls - but that was of no use either!"

"When I started gathering the animals, the RSPCA took me to Court. They insisted that I was confining wild animals against their will. They argued the accommodations were too restrictive, and it was cruel and inhumane to put so many animals into a confined space."

"Then the Environmental Agency ruled that I could not build the Ark until they'd conducted an environmental impact study on the proposed flood".

"I am still trying to resolve a complaint with the Human Rights Commission on how many minorities I am Supposed to hire for my building crew."

"Immigration is checking the Visa status of most of the people who really do want to work for me."

The Trades Union say I can't use my sons. They insist I have to hire only Union Workers and if possible with Ark-building experience."

"To make matters worse, the Inland Revenue seized all my assets, claiming I'm trying to leave the country illegally with endangered species."

"So, forgive me, Lord, but it would take me at least another 15 years for me to finish the Ark."

"Suddenly the skies cleared, the Sun began to shine and a rainbow stretched across the sky."

Noah looked-up in wonder and asked: "You mean you are not going to destroy this world? "No," said the Lord." Your Governments has done it for me."

CONCLUSION:

The present day orientation towards the Feminine and Reductionist state within all departments of life - right-hand column above, may be unique in human history - we have no way of comparing historically whether this bias will change back to a more equitable situation when both right-hand and left-hand columns above are balanced with equal or near equal puissance. This is because our sophisticated technology, a phenomenon of the present day, has consequences that engenders this bias towards all matters centripetal and set-procedures/laws (right-hand column) as argued in the texts above. There is the question also, that our present-day democracies have almost lost control; having to pass more laws to reform previous laws - put another way: [see in page 125, comment by Sir Winston Churchill] Our Democratic Systems Have Gone Somewhat Doolally! (Products of right-side column when in dominance).

I admit to being pessimistic as to whether a return to 'the otherness' or the 'blue sky' way of being (left-hand column), will ever properly return within the remaining life of the human race.

Perhaps only a terrifying catastrophe [coronavirus] can bring humanity back to a more balanced way that sees the 'bigger picture' as indicated in the left-hand column. Meanwhile we all live with fear; biting at our tails - fear that has accelerated the production and way of thinking and mind-set of the matters of the right-hand column **in extremis!** In addition, masses of women nowadays are trying to be and to act as the menfolk do consciously or unconsciously, adding to the crystallisation of the matters of the right-hand column and furthering the imbalance that dominates this epoch in human history.

However, we can rely on three things that will always
happen for humanity, and these are:

Death, Taxes, and Change.

It is the last of these three: 'Change' that will inevitably happen at some stage,
and which will alter the present day extreme ethos of the matters of the right-
hand column. How it will happen? The answer to that question lies in the hands
of the gods, or, ordained by The One God and (its) His holy omnipresence.

Having delivered the 'broadside' above about the conduct of humanity, it is important to mention its genius as well, especially on the subject of its technical and creative ability oftentimes spectacular in its brilliance and its practical applications. Such, must be balanced against the damning statements above because in engineering, medicine, and art in all their beautiful expressions, and science in all its splendid breakthroughs, not to mention sporting activities; does indeed reflect what may be called God's work, and plan. This is when humanity is immersed in its best visionary and inspired behaviour with its generosity of spirit.

There is slightly more medical ethos in the next few Essays

THERAPEUTIC PERSPECTIVE

With respect to the never-ending range and panoply of medical disorders and ailments, the Western Medicine's philosophical healing approach is not strictly correct in its application and its execution. In the round, yes, Western Medicine's scientific ethos is superb when it it comes to organ transplant and engineering us back to life and health when trauma, like being smashed-up in an automobile accident, has badly and unhappily been experienced. So too with certain virulent diseases.

The rules with Western Medicine's dealing with ailments of one sort or another, as say with Constipation, is its advocacy of the use of particular substances recommended to combat that Condition, in this respect, with Constipation, by loosening the contents of the Bowels. In other words, a nostrum that will induce the very opposite effect of the Condition in question.

The Western ethos of which I speak is one that consciously or unconsciously demonstrates the need to destroy, eliminate, and extinguish at all costs the offending disorder - the genesis of the ailment in the first place is rarely discussed, or brought to the attention of the sufferer. The modus operandi of this type of medical approach is to suppress and/or to eliminate the ailment in question.

Thus, real healing has not taken place because the **cause** of the Condition has been ignored. If there is a good result healing-wise, in truth it is so usually by default.

It is essential to understand that an ailment is an **end result** of the body's intelligence in its innate need to correct a deep **imbalance**. The **end result** is to be encouraged and fortified, in this case with the end result of Constipation.

It is the body's way to heal itself by producing Constipation, and when the body's intelligence is assisted in some way to fortify the Condition of Constipation, this very Condition is generally eliminated or displaced.

This is working with the body's intelligence and not against its capacities; contrary to the affect of most Western-style medicines; medicines so called that really are just chemico-therapies!

The treatments that align themselves with the Condition in question, in this case Constipation, are the remedies that actually induce Constipation thus assisting the body's good work by reinforcing and supporting the body's **end result**. The consequence is displacement of the Condition and its demise.

This is 'Fighting like with like'. What does this mean? The reader has probably heard the expression 'fighting fire with fire' rather as the U.S. Red Adair, deploying the same idea to fight oil and gas blow-outs by placing an explosive device as close as possible to the source of the blow-out of oil or gas already ferociously on fire, and bang! The devastating fire is rendered impotent - the oil or gas fire is extinguished.

Take two magnets. Each has a positive and a negative end. Bring the two positive ends together or the two negative ends together and they repulse, and yet these are of the same disposition but they repulse each other - such is the nature of the action of the type of medicines of which I speak. Hence fighting like with like (two engine drivers in one engine does not work. Two bosses in a marriage does not work!).

Another way of neutralising medical disorders, or Constipation in this case, is by healing the visceral organs which are the source of the Condition of Constipation in the first place. From the oriental medicine point of view, and apart from other factors, the liver and the spleen of the patient, in particular, have to be *tonified* and fortified, that is: Strengthened and brought into better balance with the other Bodily Systems - the ailment in question, Constipation, may therefore be extinguished. Though, the following is simplistic, look to anger and/or frustration with the Liver and look to worry and/or pensiveness with the Spleen.

In truth, as with *Aryuvedic* Medicine, a process of cleansing, which is a kind of detoxification, should be the first port of call, so to speak, whether with the administration of herbal remedies (possibly in homeopathic form), or with bodywork type therapies as with Shiatsu, Acupuncture, Osteopathy, Craniosacral Therapy and more.

It may be stated that any of these therapies have a purging effect as well as a powerful healing result, especially with the addition and the administration of certain herbal substances to cleanse the soma.

Then there is self-bodywork (very powerful). This is the immersing of oneself deep into the ancient disciplinary practices such as with Tai Chi; Chi Kung; Hatha Yoga; Do-in.

The body is constructed in such a way as to require daily exercise, if this daily activity is ignored, the body will slowly atrophy. Stress, and emotional stress are dealt with best, with these regimens apart from prayer and meditation.

These dynamic and galvanising disciplines mentioned above assist the cleansing of the body/mind, as well as the strengthening the interior visceral organs.

Thus, the confrontations life enjoys throwing at our feet are more easily dealt with, because we are stronger and better able to endure much more rigour than is usual as the excellent effects of these practices change for good our vulnerable interiors.

Movement of the body, its limbs and its spine is essential for health. Motion moves blood and fluids around the body and assists keeping the whole System cleansed, oxygenated and nourished - necessary to maintain health throughout life - not to mention that movement assists articulation of all the bodily joints. Work-outs at the gymnasium and other forms of exercise are good and better than no exercise at all.

However, these strengthen the outer body and its muscular systems, and do very little for the body interior leaving visceral organs as weak as ever. It is the reinforcing of the strength of the body's visceral organs that ultimately bestows good health.

IT IS THE FUNCTION OF A GOOD THERAPIST AS A *CHI* ENGINEER/ PRANA MECHANIC TO ASSIST THE BODY TO ENABLE IT TO INCREASE ITS LIFE FORCE (*CHI*) AND HEALTH, BY NATURAL MEANS. ALL CHEMICAL SUPPRESSING MEDICINE DIMINISHES THIS LIFE FORCE - THEY DO NOT HEAL.

UNDERSTANDING THE AFTER-EFFECTS RESULTING FROM ALTERNATIVE MEDICAL TREATMENTS

When suffering a given medical Condition we may be in the habit of thinking that we can obtain a 'quick-fix' to remedy it, and consequently all will be well!

1. Re-actions to the reception of Alternative Medical Treatment including Bodywork may give rise to physical discomfort and discomposure and some mental and emotional anxiety. This experience by the patient may be felt particularly following the first and the second treatments.

2. Physiologically the body will be undergoing an interesting change: The treatments would have initiated a process whereby elements within it begin to 'push and to pull' the various operations of the organs of the body hopefully, returning them to function more harmoniously and in better balance with one another.

3. The process is also one of cleansing and detoxifying on both a physical and a psychological level, and as stated above may not be so pleasant to endure – but 'running the gauntlet' in this way will pay dividends in the end, health-wise. Disagreeable manifestations, physical and emotional, may be discussed with the Therapist concerned.

4. Perhaps a minimum of six treatments will be required to 'turn the corner' so to speak, to enjoy the eventual demise and dissolution of the ailment in question.

5. It should be born in mind that allopathic remedies prescribed by your doctors serve only to change or to eliminate the Symptoms of your Disorder – actually they do not cure that ailment - if they do, it is usually by default! Indeed they may well have driven that disorder further into your Physiological System whose ramifications manifest at a later date as a medical problem that could even be worse than the original problem; altogether therefore, being more weakening and debilitating to your health. The probability now is that you may have to deal with, and to endure the consequences of these earlier ill-advised directions as additions to the first disorder you suffered.

6. It is without doubt that when we suffer any form of illness or irksome Condition, and even being 'out of sorts' that our 'Energetic' life-force (*Chi*) is at a low-ebb, especially so, if there is an organic problem within the body as well. These deficiencies may be the first manifestations of a fateful illness to come!

7. In truth, and as we know, a balanced lifestyle including wholesome habits, unpolluted thinking and feeling, and harmonious surroundings, maintain and indeed improve health.

8. Of course all this is difficult to achieve, and to carry-out, yet we know intuitively what to do, what to take, what to attain, and how to be – what some might call: The articles and the fruit of our natural inheritance!

9. We do have to begin from some point and to build-up our health bit by bit. Thus, it is possible to enjoy this purer way of life – life unsatisfactorily described in modern times by some scientists as 'just a group of chemical compounds'.

10. Confidentially, this way of thinking about creation as just a group 'Chemicals' is perhaps one of the most damaging of our human mistakes, and way of thinking, because the **sacredness** and the **mystery** of existence is squeezed into oblivion, causing confusion and limitations in all departments of life and interestingly dismantling human spiritual instinct.

11. It is this extraordinary mystery that we all possess within us, and it has many levels of manifestation - from the highest and lofty to the lowest and mundane. That is, from the ethereal, to the temporal. It is the *Chi** of living existence (it is your *chi* reading this!). There are different grades of *Chi* from the diaphanous and nebulous to the most physically coarse - all having their place within the human construct as well as directing the template of life generally.

12. This exquisite ethereal *Chi* substance in its many roles within our bodies is injured and damaged, depending on the intensity of toxic substances absorbed, by the daily use of prescribed drugs offered by our doctors and sponsored by government.

13. The narcotics taken by those who are generally interiorly disturbed, and who suffer an absence of a stable **foundation,** and who are generally feckless, and work-shy, will most definitely have to endure, in addition to other health issues, absence of being grounded.

14. The use of narcotics are mostly ingested by us out of context (See Alexander's Essay above: Alcohol, A Non-Orthodox View).

15. All these drugs both legitimate and non-legitimate badly affect our physiology and therefore our psychological health. They do not cure, they merely suppress, and as stated above manifesting later into another kind of illness or illnesses.

Chi* - Chinese. *Qi* - Japanese: Is the carrier wave that holds the universe together and everything living therein.

Purity matters in body, mind and emotions. Of course, illnesses occur with the best of us, however, recovery is fast and enduring with proper thoughts, moderate living and acceptance of what is. Change yourself and the world will change. The madness of the world, more than ever now, is a pure reflection of the inner state of humanity as it is in this present very dangerous epoch.

The present day attitude of unwholesome thinking amongst the many seems to be a Western World phenomenon, but this phenomenon insidiously contaminates other peoples' thinking and feeling in various parts of the Globe. It is no wonder there exists around the world so much illness, neurosis and consequent psychosis – however, sanity, actually, is just a hair's-breadth away!

*The bodywork offered at our Harrow Clinic (alexalign.uk@gmail.com) in its many aspects may miraculously put you back into balance and help restore your **Chi** to function more healthily. If you desire to be at your optimum state of health, look to your diet, your attitude to life, your attitude to yourself, your attitude to others. Whether you exercise sufficiently, whether your living circumstances are conducive to a balanced lifestyle.*

All these things, including what you eat may be discussed with your Therapist, and do take into consideration: Honi soit qui mal y pence. (Evil to him who thinks evil).

FURTHER: You may begin your quest by keeping your body warm. Do not allow circumstances to place you into wind, cold and dampness.

All these conditions play havoc with your physiology and subsequently produce a weakening to your immune system. Drink warm drinks and eat cooked food. Use iron or steel cooking pots. Reduce sweet stuffs and increase vegetable food. Never use a microwave oven!

Eat organic food when and where you can. Stop all wine and spirit abuse. Stop all smoking. Without knowing it, you are slowly killing yourself if you do not adhere to these basic tenets.

Very few doctors of medicine recognise the sacred life force Chi that is so deranged by our wholesale use of prescribed drugs and which damage our Chi's power thereby injuring our vital organs. This Chi is most delicate and has limitations and is likened to the quality of an atmosphere. That is, the Chi within a cathedral is quite different to that of the Chi of the inside of a prison. So too, the Chi within a bordello is different from the Chi within a concert hall for classical music. There is good chi and bad chi. Bad chi is called: 'Sha' in Chinese. Never over eat - we eat too much. In truth this is the cause of obesity.

This is what is so delicate, you cannot necessarily touch Chi but you feel its affect, and as such, the Chi of our bodies is fragile and may be destroyed all at once - death, or slowly by disease. Of course prescribed drugs have their place - they may be necessary in so many cases to maintain life as a priority. This is when these allopathic substances have their true value.

ADVICE TO PATIENTS AS STATED
ABOVE REPEATED HERE

USE WARMTH WHENEVER YOU CAN - WE ARE TOO
COLD TEMPERATURE-WISE INTERIORLY

LEAVE-OFF ALLOPATHIC DRUGS THAT DEPLETE THE SYSTEM AND
REDUCE *CHI*. BEGIN A PROCESS OF ELIMINATING THEIR USE - ONLY TAKE
OR DO WHEN NOTHING ELSE WORKS. SO TOO WITH SURGERY. NEVER
USE MICROWAVE OVENS - USAGE DEPLETES BLOOD VITALITY

NEVER USE ALUMINIUM COOKING UTENSILS

INCREASE YOUR GREENS AND DECREASE YOUR SWEET ITEMS INCLUDING FRUITS

BUY ORGANIC WHERE YOU CAN

CHECK-OUT **SIRT** AND **KETOGENIC** DIET

USE GINGER INTERNALLY AND EXTERNALLY EVERYDAY - IDEALLY ORGANIC

USE TURMERIC ALSO BUT COOKED

IF THREE MEALS A DAY ARE EATEN, TWO SHOULD BE
COOKED. REDUCE RAW FOOD EATING

CHEW FOOD - DIGESTION BEGINS IN THE MOUTH

**Post Script: As stated above: Yes there are times when drugs and/or surgery
are necessary but these must always be adopted as the last resort. What matters
is to increase your 'Chi', your life force that is fundamental to healthy living.
Increasing 'Chi'; this delicate but powerful ethereal energy that permeates and
sustains all of life, but is also The Carrier Wave that holds the Universe together,
may be improved upon by the recommendations above, but also by the powerful
bodywork as recommended already, and such as with the oriental medicinal
approaches as carried-out within the walls of our Harrow U.K. Clinic.**

THE CONFLICT THAT HAS ALWAYS EXISTED BETWEEN MALE AND FEMALE IS NOT CONFINED ONLY TO MAN VERSUS WOMAN OR WOMAN VERSUS MAN, BUT EXTENDS TO ALL AND EVERYTHING IN EXISTENCE BOTH IN OBJECT AND IN SUBJECT

CONSIDER THE FOLLOWING:

(Some repetition of previous texts).

1. The Feminine aspect naturally demands proof or evidence of the ramifications of a Subject or of an Object. The nature of this demand is in the form of calibration, examination, and for its parts be notated and listed, proven and more. This is because the Feminine is linked to Earth, Formulation, Discipline, Tradition, Science, Matter, Moon and '*Yin*' and looks to the mundane and the practical, and is a perfectly proper viewpoint.

2. The Masculine aspect of the ramifications of a Subject or of an Object tends to be conceptual and therefore Revelation, Inspiration, Illumination, Transcendence, Theory, and the wisdom of the ages (interior & exterior wisdom) brings into being, knowledge of the 'bigger picture' without the employment of scientific laboratories to **'prove'** the topic under discussion. This is because the Masculine is linked to Heaven, Force, Metaphysics, 'Energetics', Sun and '*Yang*' and in essence represent, and from which issue, the **original plans** of 'All & Everything', and is also a perfect viewpoint.

These Male and Female energies or forces act as a thread that binds 'All and Everything' together in concert. That is: Every <u>Object</u> and every <u>Subject</u> in our living existence is controlled by this **Male and Female Law** and indeed is permeated by it.

The **Law** of these two forces, Male & Female is inextricably linked, as it is in the animation of the DNA chain, and as it is in the Wave (Masculine) and in the Particle (Feminine). Nothing may come into being without the interplay, warp and woof of these two energies, these two forces Masculine and Feminine.

Most of us are unable to be objective, for whatever reason, sufficient to enable the essential perceiving of two seemingly opposed points of view, Masculine & Feminine as being two parts of a whole, and therefore complementary.

The topic of Alternative Medicine v. Orthodox Medicine explains well the statements above and I am repeating this subject but with some added material.

Trauma aside, which is usually dealt with admirably by scientifically based **Orthodox Medicine,** Orthodox Medicine's ethos is such that it requires experimentation with substances, usually to allay or quash pathological symptoms presented by the patient, but also the cutting-out, or the cutting-off, of the offending part that belongs to that patient - that body part that happens to be bad, offensive, ailing and just a plain nuisance!

Experimentation is usually performed in the scientific laboratory, whose aim is to find a way to eliminate an illness, post-haste, but also to name and notate it and to find a Substance to cure it. In reality, it is a Substance that will merely assist in eliminating the Symptoms of a pathological Condition – a cure does not really come into the equation, if it does, it is usually by default.

By understanding the explanations given above, it will be perceived by the reader of this article that **Orthodox Medicine** is a **Feminine application** to the practice of Medicine, requiring absolute diagnosis of the ailment in question and the detailed ways in which it is to be exercised.

With **Alternative Medicine,** its ethos is diametrically opposite to that of Orthodox Medicine's modus operandi as the 'bigger picture' is taken into consideration when accessing the pathological model the patient Presents.

The requirement is to question life-style and habits of the patient; their energetic presentation, i.e. body-language and the perceptions of the Therapist as to the patient's overall aura or light or non-light as the case may be, emanating or not emanating from them.

Most of us, therapist or laymen, may intuit the Condition of a patient by this exudation or non-exudation of light and quality of energy (*Chi*), that says so much. The Therapist may now make deductions as to how treatment should be applied and as to the type of treatment plan to be implemented.

There are, of course, more specific ways of diagnosing the pathological disorder by Alternative Medical means (mostly ways which are born out of Oriental Medicine) by the Therapist, but the way just described is one that dares not to speak its name because of the current scientific obsession to measure All and Everything to exactitude and to the point where we are all driven to distraction and tedium.

The spiritual and the higher cultivated centres in us all, do determine to a large extent the kind of pathologies, if any, that will manifest during our life's development – these, so important, are not usually taken into consideration by Orthodox Medicine as many of us know.

By understanding the interpretations given above, it will be ascertained by the reader of this Essay that **Alternative Medicine** is a **Masculine application** to the practice of Medicine, requiring a universal appraisal to the ailment in question and the taking into consideration of the long term effects of its treatment models.

Depending on the type of disorder the patient suffers, both Alternative and Orthodox Medicine have their place, and in 50% of instances an Orthodox approach is best, and in the other 50% of instances Alternative Medicine may be the better approach to deploy altogether, meaning legitimacy of, and accepting the two sides to a medical issue without bias, this eclectic methodology.

Another example of two points of view follows:-

THE STUPENDOUS TOPIC OF THIS DIGITAL AGE AND THE INTERNET IN PARTICULAR

(The Male and Female aspects are presented according to the arguments put forth by these Essays)

It is extraordinary that with this spectacular development with Science, we human beings are able to enjoy a form of extraordinary communication of all kinds, usually within seconds of time with other human beings of whatever ilk across the whole globe, thus shrinking it, in a sense, by bringing us homo sapiens into one family.

Some people might say that this technological progress is a brilliant aspect of God's Mind manifesting through the ingenuity of a few brilliant human minds.

Perhaps it is part of a long-term plan that is the Creator's purpose!

Simultaneously, it is a terrible indictment on us, mankind, that aspects of the Internet have been commandeered for criminal activities - criminal activities, in truth, that are almost impossible to control. As usual the felons amongst us rely on the gullibility and the innocents of the majority of people, running rings around the authorities and who are able to dodge in so many cases those who are assigned to police the Net.

It is said by wise teachers of old, that with any new development, its silent shadow follows and this is not obvious until things begin to change, often for the worst, as the new development gains momentum.

This is the hidden part already mentioned above in this Book and which has the function of either destroying that new development, or by making it stronger through the process of it being confronted by this kind of negative friction, and thus this new development is made more 'water-tight' so to speak.

The beautiful lotus flower feeds off the dregs within the sullied water it floats on - the more filthy the contents of the water, the richer and bigger the plant and its flower.

Horrible as it is, the criminals amongst us have their place, acting in a sense as The Devil's Advocates. Thus, we as ordinary people are forced to wake-up in becoming more wary of life and living which ultimately has to be to our advantage.

The 'new idea' that is usually altruistic is Solar, Male and *Yang*. The difficulties and the realism of what will follow is Lunar, Female and *Yin* according to the precepts as outlined above within a number of these Essays.

ESSENTIAL GUIDE NOTES TO ASSIST ALIGNMENT OF PELVIS AND SPINE TO REDUCE AND EVEN ELIMINATE BACK-PAIN AND THEREFORE ALL OTHER MUSCULOSKELETAL ACHES & PAINS

The relevance of the Acid/Alkaline balance of the fluids within the body:

Most of us eat more acid forming foods than alkaline forming foods - habit! This way of eating tends to engender excess acidity within the fluids of the body including the blood itself. The imbalance is potentially detrimental to our health because it means an acidic build-up that may damage in time our bones, joints, ligaments, tendons, muscles and other body tissues.

Our physiological system of checks and balances within the body is put under great strain in neutralising excess acid build-up - the body neutralises excess acid inefficiently when overwhelmed with acidic producing foods. The physiological intelligence within the body will push excess residues of these acids away from the vital organs, and what it cannot eject through bodily wastage, will deliver the remnants or residues of this waste to the bony joints and other related structures. The malefic effects are as follows:

MESENTERY - this internal abdominal structure is weakened when it has absorbed toxic residues such as to cause it to sag and swell and because of this it tends to protrude (beer belly). Also the abnormal pulling forward of a balloon-like heavy belly may engender a lordosis of the lumbar spine weakening the lumbar spinal segments in the process. In addition, this abnormality may have detrimental consequences to the other segments of the spine. Prolapsed visceral organs as with the intestines are also important factors to consider with the weakening of the abdominal cavity.

INTERVERTEBRAL DISCS (cartilage) - may physically contract and harden thus lessening mobility and flexibility of the segments of the spine leading to stiffness and pain and the horrible potential of the rupturing of an intervertebral disc.

LIGAMENTS - when these absorb acid residues, they may become weak, brittle and contracted and therefore they will lose their flexibility and so distortion of bony joints and subluxations is inevitable because these ligaments are attached to relevant bone. In fact it means that this ligamental impairment must have a deleterious affect on all the bony joints of the whole spine and also therefore the sacroiliac joints.

MUSCLES - excess acid residues may be injurious to various muscle systems. Some muscles becoming too tight and stiff and others becoming too soft and flaccid. This places an extra strain on the bony joints of the whole anatomical frame and so dislocation of these junction points may occur - commonly the bony articulations of the pelvis and all weight-bearing joint-hinges suffer - hyper-mobility of a joint will cause abnormality of movement and so the whole skeletal frame may suffer.

OSTEOPOROSIS - acidity may leach-out mineral calcium from the body complex, and with the bones especially - we need to be aware of the serious consequences to the weakening strength of the bones when this occurs.

THE BONY SPINAL SEGMENTS (vertebrae) - it is not only the intervertebral disc that deteriorates as mentioned above, but also the spinal segment itself is in detriment. They, the vertebral segments, may shrink and harden, enough to lessen the size of the foramina (small openings) that are at the root of the spinal processes and through which pass the relevant nerve fibres. In this way, groups of nerve fibres are constricted and cannot move (they require a small amount of movement back and forth) - thus, they the nerve fibres, are being abnormally compressed and restricted in movement.

Because of this, pain and problematic effects to all structures including the visceral organs may occur and so they may become deficient in their functions because the electrical and biological impulses which these fibres conduct, will do so in an abnormal and in a limited way. The twelve cranial nerves may not escape this scenario of dysfunction either.

Avoiding the body-interior debacle as outlined above, it would be wise to lessen the intake of acid producing foods and to increase the consumption of alkaline producing foods such as with vegetables and certain grains but preferably organic in origin. Log-onto: naturalhealthschool.com

ENVISAGE THE HUMAN SPINE AS A METAL SPRING/COIL

Picture the human spine as a strong flexible metal spring that may be bent virtually in all directions (up and down as well as side to side) and capable of contraction, expansion and torsion clockwise and anti-clockwise. The spine's intervertebral discs endow it with this capability of springiness. Its tensile strength exists because of the three specialised ligaments threading through and holding the vertebrae and the intervertebral discs against one another into their correct positions.

It is in the nature of this construct to enjoy safe osteopathic adjustments when segments have marginally become misaligned and corrective procedures administered.

By electing to choose a useful form of exercise or discipline (see below), which bends and contorts this magnificent tensile spring, the spine, you are loosening and dispersing acid residues and any sediment trapped and stuck within the structures of the vertebral joints of your spine. Thus, you are assisting it to maintain its health by keeping it clean and free of inflexibility. There is a commensurate increase in blood flow and therefore nourishment both to the discs and those very spinal segments.

The Pelvic Corrector Device when used to re-adjust the pelvis and spine is the most perfect way of giving maintenance to the spine thereby helping it return back to its pristine state. (www.alexaligntherapies.com)

In addition to these 'workouts', it may be understood now why any kind of bodywork, strong massage particularly on and over the spine, will be beneficial as they help to keep the spine supple. In the author's opinion, Shiatsu is probably the most powerful and best form of bodywork that may be enjoyed and revered !

Since 'bodywork' can assist this type of detoxification of the physiological body, a discomforting re-action may occur especially the following day, but it is worth 'running the gauntlet' in this way..

Undertaking a discipline such as with Hatha Yoga (Hat-Yog), Tai Chi, Chi Kung, means that you have cleansed your body sufficiently to enjoy, for example Shiatsu treatments as mentioned above without a discombobulating discomforting re-action.

Put another way: subsequent fall-out after the 'nuclear explosion' of a treatment, and because you already practice a 'discipline', in this way a difficult re-action is unlikely to be suffered.

Though The Alexander Technique (no relationship to the author or to Pelvic Correction) and Pilates are excellent disciplines, only those ancient practices mentioned above strengthen the interior body, that is mainly: the visceral organs. Workouts at gymnasiums (Gym) are alright, but these only strengthen the outer body - the interior body remains weak.

SMOKING

In addition to the damage caused by smoking to our lungs, it has been proven by research and observation that smoking, which includes the smoking of narcotics, engenders the fine network of blood vessels within the vertebral segments of the spine to contract in size. This is very undesirable, because the way to keep intervertebral discs healthy and with inherent springiness is for them to take their nourishment from their adjacent vertebral segments.

The narrowing of these fine blood vessels, restricting blood flow tends to disable the process of supply, so the vertebral segments suffer and in turn so do these intervertebral discs and subsequently, the whole spine deteriorates over time.

When a human stands erect, compression of the intervertebral discs takes place and when a human lies-down, his intervertebral discs swell somewhat because they are receiving nourishment (blood) from their adjacent spinal segments (vertebrae).

Therefore, in addition to a regular night's sleep, it is recommended for him/her to enjoy a 'siesta' sometime during the day. The health of the spine should improve.

Hanging upside-down, using an inversion machine should now be seen as beneficial as well - the stretch opens-up the whole of the spinal construct. Also undertaking the so-called 'chin-up' that is, dangling your body free, by using your hands to hold firmly a support bar of sorts will have a similar favourable effect.

THE HEALTH OF THE COLON IS INVOLVED IN MAINTAINING A STABLE PELVIS

It is more than likely that a large percentage of us suffer with the interior fungal infection of Candida. The body's immune system cannot always cope with this parasitic entity, indeed, Candida might be thought of as a pestilential plague of sorts.

It affects us, mentally, emotionally and physically in a destructive way.

To maintain a modicum of health in life, for which we have to fight and to struggle to do so, lessens the joy of living it. Mind you, there are a few strange Beings, who wallow in this kind of suffering - it takes all sorts as it is said!

The ill-affects of Candida may well be the reason behind certain inconvenient food allergies some of us experience. We may include in this as well the adverse re-action to pollen floating in the air breathed-in.

There may also be a vaccination element, amongst other things, giving rise to the rejection of certain food stuffs and particular abnormal behaviours suffered by the young especially. That is, the possible consequent deleterious effect of inoculations forced on us in childhood.

Candida's greatest felons are injuries to the Colon; its main place of residence. Possessing a 'sweet tooth' is a handicap which ideally should be addressed very seriously as to its necessary diminution. The health and strength of the Colon most definitely has a profound effect on the stability of the bony pelvis, amongst other things as it is an inseparable component of its structure and its purpose.

Probably the most natural antidote to candida is the proper use of formidable garlic (the wonder vegetable). Best consumed cooked, as raw garlic may engender inconvenient diarrhoea. Garlic pearls (pills) are acceptable, but the actual raw clove is best but cooked. Honey mixed with prepared raw garlic cloves may be eaten together without having to cook the garlic itself.

BACK POCKET SCIATICA AND COLD WINDY WEATHER

Placing a wallet or such like into your back pocket should be avoided, because as you sit, the horizontality of the pelvis may be seriously compromised. Also this forced posture may place abnormal pressure onto the piriformis muscle at the ball and socket joint of the hip, thus contributing to pelvic misalignment.

It is recommended that you maintain a covered abdomen (belly) and lower back lumbar region at all times. It is said that the kidneys loath cold and chill. Their efficient functioning is vital for healthy bones and maintenance of strength and the **Will** to do.

According to Chinese Medicine Lore, they hold our money in the bank energy-wise; in simple terms they are our batteries and supply power to the rest of the visceral organs of our bodies. Keep your belly (Hara) and your lower back warm at all times. Do not follow ridiculous and stupid fashion that tends to produce garments that expose our most precious parts, abdomen and lumbar, to all and sundry including to cold, windy and wet weather.

Lifting any object, weighty or otherwise, should be performed without a twisting motion - always be square-on to the object you lift, and you may avoid your back giving-way engendering pain and the depressing thought that you have suddenly aged 20 years.

**Actually, there is no food substance that has an absolute value acid/alkaline-wise.
Some people need more acid producing foods than alkaline producing foods according to
their body type. Log-on to: naturalhealthschool.com
for the science and more behind the theory.**

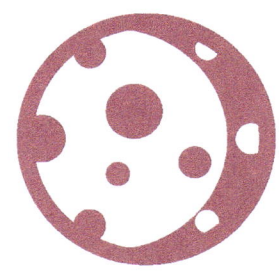

ALL FOR ONE AND ONE FOR ALL

Confusion and perplexity exists with the execution of fairness and balance by those who might have power over us, such as with authority as exercised, by our politicians for example. Many politicians not all of course, suffer the certainty of giving recognition and favour to the **Many** and barely an acknowledgment and assistance to the **One**.

*The object of this written piece is to clarify and elucidate the contents of the ancient laws (outlined below) that explain the correctness of the human gratifying of giving to the **one** and simultaneously the human gratifying of giving to the **many**, thereby establishing a perfect balance between these two opposing **forces**: which is to the **one** and to the **many**. This has to include with this contrary phenomena not only when they are in abstraction, that is: In thought, but also when put into practical action. That is:*

The giving to the One as opposed to the giving to the Many, but equal in weight, deed and importance to each other.

With respect to the memory of the late Right Honourable Anthony Wedgwood Benn (Tony Ben as he preferred to be called), gave the impression always that he loved and respected the many and was not particularly interested too much in the needs of the one. Indeed, it is possible that the more he loved humanity, the more he disliked the individual! The aphorism: 'All for one and one for all' is very fine but rarely implemented, there is almost always bias towards one end of this spectrum and not to its polar opposite end!

The Industrial Unions have this inherent dichotomy which is: how much attention and succour should be given to an individual Member as opposed to the needs of all the individuals en mass, as Members of that Union?

The expression: Charity Begins At Home......its meaning nowadays seems to be gathering serious thought and engendering the anger born of unfairness that the home or indigenous population perceives and experiences. It is angry particularly with those individuals in high positions bent on sending enormous amounts of money abroad to countries that squander it, and most of whom actually hate or dislike the country that is doing the giving.

Most of the donees consider that the donor countries suffer with sentimentality and feebleness in their ridiculous attempts to show their compassion.

What has this to do with: the **One** as opposed to the **Many**?
Scale-up the **One** and the **Many** and we have a similar disparity as follows:

THE **NATIONAL (One)** TRIBAL FAMILY AS OPPOSED TO THE **INTERNATIONAL (Many)** GROUP OF FAMILIES!

So much money is sent abroad when so much of that money is desperately needed at Home. The politics of the matter has and is and does create a terrible imbalance when equality is absent between the needs of the **one** and the needs of the **many.**

Much of that squandered money rarely goes to where it is supposed to go. Dictators and psychopaths in powerful positions spirit away much of it for their own aggrandisement. The clever but dead lunatic Yasser Arafat purloined $900,000,000.00 to his own bank accounts abroad - much of this money meant for his Palestinian people, though he was in fact Egyptian by birth.

Projects that the money is supposed to fund, do not come into being or do so lacking purpose and function. Also, what money is sent is never enough - cupidity and greed is commonplace! Saddam Husain once said that he knows his people in that: 'If I give them an inch, they will take a yard' - but that is true of much of humanity anyway! In Arafat's case, we have favour to the **one** to the detriment of the **many.**

The Ancient Laws referred to in the first paragraph above are as follows:

Within astrological lore, two of the twelve Signs of the Zodiac, suffering polarity within the astrological construct are Capricorn opposing Cancer. (A circle is given 360º. Each astrological sign traditionally is given a 30º calibration. Twelve Signs x Thirty degrees = 360º. Within this circle, these two astrological signs Capricorn and Cancer are exactly 180º in opposition to each other). Their planetary monarchs are Saturn ruling the Sign of Capricorn and Earth's Moon ruling the Sign of Cancer.

The twelve Astrological Signs reflect all possible aspects of creation both in abstraction and in manifestation.

The two Signs in question, Capricorn and Cancer represent 2/12's of creation's matrix. The matrix is creation's spectacular diversity all contained within the 12 departments of life (Astrological Signs/Houses) here and beyond.

In creation and for us humans, the Capricorn Sign mode through its Monarch Saturn is to insure the continuance of law and order, no matter how painful. Justice is for all and jurisprudence too. In addition, all those items and subjects that possess gravity and important meaning such as with: governance; accountancy; science; engineering; mathematics; Construction; medicine and much more are governed by planet Saturn expressed through the Capricorn Sign.

Therefore, all these subjects have to do with the **Many;** in that they cover durability and security for the masses. The Capricorn modus operandi refers to all that is orthodox and establishes

Tradition to enable **continuity** and a semblance of **stability** in this unstable world. As regards to gender, this mode now becomes Solar, *Yang*, Masculine, Centrifugal, and outgoing in nature.

In creation and for us humans, the Cancer Sign mode through its Monarch the Moon is to ensure that there is a strong measure of cohesion within the immediate family unit. Within the closest family ethos, a kind of domestic wisdom and common sense should be present which assists the ties of blood. According to astrological lore, and so too in many religions, the Moon's influence and importance actuates all things. As regards to gender, this mode is Lunar, *Yin*, Feminine, Centripetal.

That is: nothing in or on Earth can come into being or be stable without the Moon's influence/function that will manifest through the Sign of Cancer. It marks-out the time for things to manifest. Hence, the New Moons and the Full Moons initiate the beginnings of high holy and festival days in many Faiths.

The menstruation cycle within women. The seasons' beginnings in the growth of the vegetal world and the decay, the actions and behaviour of animals, the sanity or non sanity of us Homo sapiens!......and much more.

It may be understood now that the Moon's influence is mainly for **ones own group and near environment**, but also for all things flitting and ephemeral as for example: routine daily/weekly/monthly events etc., The Capricorn/Saturn influence is much more profound and wide and covers all those things that endure, protect and obtain for humanity as a whole.

If you happen to meet a local councillor, he or she might be very helpful in dealing with your domestic or community problem. Visit his/her house, and the councillor's spouse might complain to you privately how the home matters are neglected in favour of the people of the town the councillor has jurisdiction over.

The children do not get sufficient attention and nor does he/she. The councillor is advocate to the **many** to the detriment of the **one**!

This is:

THE **PERSONAL (One)** FAMILY, AS OPPOSED TO THE
NATIONAL (Many) FAMILY AS A TRIBAL GROUP

It was probably similar domestically with the great Mahatma Gandhi of India. It is believed that his family suffered in a number of ways due to his political standing and worldly obsession with the bigger issues of the day. His convictions were to advocate for the **many** forgetting about the **one**? Read: **The Mail on Sunday** 10/2/19 on and about Jeremy Corbyn.

The mass migration within the present epoch is catastrophic but interesting nevertheless. Being overwhelmed by a crisis that is disastrous to a nation which engenders a mass exit of that nation or a large percentage of it, has insoluble difficulties for the host nations that allow absorption of these homeless and hapless members of the neurotic human race.

Forced onto governments of various nations that have inadvertently become host nations, the migrants, almost automatically are given resources to enable them to survive, usually to the detriment of home or indigenous populations within the host countries. So by force of events almost beyond control, the **many** is in favour opposed to the **one** who is not - just the scale is larger.

Further, there exists an automatic imbalance of precious resources when a greater percentage of these assets are given to the **many** to the detriment of the **one.**

The **many** in this case being the migrants from foreign countries and the native peoples being the **one**. See the Heading above reproduced here:

> THE **NATIONAL** TRIBAL FAMILY (**One** and is a feature of the Sign of Cancer) AS OPPOSED TO THE **INTERNATIONAL** GROUP OF FAMILIES (**Many** and is a feature of the Sign of Capricorn).

Footnote to the migrant debacle:

It has become, in modern times, the norm to take care of refugees political and otherwise. Usually they are taken-in by naive thinking countries. Countries relatively civilised from the Western viewpoint, and believing that as human beings they (the refugees) are the same in mentality as everyone else. Great mistake! It will cost lives and capital, damaging economies taking-in people whose mindset and culture is diametrically opposed to the host nations'. It is courting the most terrible danger as may already be seen and will be seen and experienced sufficient to cause panic throughout our sentimental Western World. The truth about Brexit as voted by the many (the demos) in Britain reflected the underlying fear of being overwhelmed by people (refugees) of a totally different ethos that could damage a way of life - a way of life that by and large works well enough and took a thousand years or more to attain and that has relative stability.

Even in recent history, the royal families of the European countries (royal families now mostly defunct sadly) had their nasty and virulent differences. (Life of Edward VIII?).

Exacerbated by the psychotic behaviour of Kaiser Wilhelm of Germany, and as such his conduct giving rise to great consternation amongst his royal relatives, actually helped engender Europe to be shunted into a terrifying direction previously unforeseen (First World War). This is an affect of a minority driving the destiny of a majority - the **one** as opposed to the **many**.

Then we have differences and urgencies within epochs in human history that require a dictatorship of sorts to enable essential things to be carried-out to resolve major issues at speed, that would only, under a democracy, making decisions, cause delay and confusion.

A declaration of War must produce a War Cabinet to undertake immediate important decisions for the nation's survival, without employing the madnesses (in this dire situation) of dithering democratic governments only to bring about in there deliberations: feeble and cowardly decisions.

Strong and powerful dictatorship with directives is required as a priority rising above everything else in importance. This is also an example of the **one** leading the **many**.

To understand, to comprehend the essence of this Essay will enable the reader to enjoy the significance of the meaning and purpose of The Tribe, The Gang, The football team when The Moon as Monarch of the Sign of Cancer, expresses itself as the cogent: Mother, Queen Bee, and Matriarch, and the familial compulsion, The Gang, The Tribe etc., to rally round Her.

By so doing, **safety and security** is experienced by the members of that family but also it is a given that there is an essential sense of **belonging** to it and being **nurtured** by it. Thus, the **one** is emphasised as opposed to the **many**.

In this way, it may be understood how powerful belonging to a group, tribe and team is, usually to the point of hostilities regularly manifesting, towards: **The Other Group**, closing-off the bigger, grander picture that in truth, we all belong to, which is: The **Many.**

This explains the disregard, the loathing, the aspersions thrown at larger foreign groups that often seem to be given greater favour by our and other grouped government co-ordinated actions.

The Earth's Moon may be seen to be active and to influence the physical and mental faculties within people and nations.

Observe the mass movement of crowds of people within a football stadium. They move their bodies in the same coordinated rhythm. Individuality has ceased to be.

They are all in the thrall of a force that cannot be controlled, exactly as the tides cannot be directed as they are moved by the power of the Moon. The movement of the crowds referred to above, should remind us of undulating water as they, the people move in collaboration. **One** is dominant.

It may now be understood how mass hysteria may be observed when an event so powerful affects millions of people in an absurd way as when Princess Diana died in an automobile accident. How could so many people be so distressed about a person 99% of whom they had never met? The power of image, basically superficial that seems to have so much puissance, says much about us homo sapiens species nowadays! This is the **one** affecting the **many**.

Footnote to the Princess Diana phenomenon:

Another possible explanation as to the mass grief felt by so many people; in that the unconscious mind was shown how easy it was for a famous and illustrious human-being could be snuffed-out of existence in such an undignified way, had created the interior terror within us that reflected the idea that a lesser human-being could easily die in the same useless way - the mass grief felt at the time was grief *actually for oneself. That is: the horrible realisation as to how vulnerable **I** am and that there by the grace of God go **I**.*

Further, a whole nation, brainwashed into a mindset that can be influenced to murder and to kill any other group or individual that does not conform to a formula that has been taught to that nation. A formula that has been accepted to be the true one, that is the only right and proper way of being, and is superior to any other, as was manifest in 1930/1940's Germany, can undertake actions that to many of us are incomprehensible. Then humanness and civility disappear with this kind of appalling Conditioning. Again, the **many** are subjugated by the **one**.

Footnote to the subject outlined above:

*As regards 'brainwashing', our mode of bringing-up children suffers this fate with virtually all of us as human-beings. We behave and think in a similar or the same way as do our parents in most cases. Many readers will be wondering whether the emphasis on the **ONE** is a Masculine or a Feminine demarcation, but also whether the emphasis on the **MANY** is a Masculine or a Feminine demarcation according to the contents of a few of the Essays above? The bigger, grander picture of the **MANY** is Masculine and that of the smaller family group of **ONE** is Feminine. Our religious bringing-up and its heavy conditioning determines how many of us will behave in a certain predictable manner, and the more extreme and the more disciplined that religion is, the more we are subject to its control even if many of its precepts are flawed especially in modern times. The problem is that the conditioning may be so overwhelming that nothing can get through, so to speak, even with perfect reasoning revealing the bigger-picture. That is: The more universal and less divisive the approach, may still be rejected because our heavily conditioned minds direct us to the contrary.*

In conclusion, this Essay explains just one aspect of creation - the One and the Many. Their natural opposition may be explained according to the small number of cosmic laws as outlined above. Ideally they should be in balance 50/50 to help eliminate or reduce objections from either side.

THE ESSAYS FOLLOWING THIS PAGE HAVE TO DEAL WITH MANY SUBJECTS BUT ALL ELUCIDATE THE DEEPER AND MORE FUNDAMENTAL INNER MEANINGS OF THE TERMS OF *YIN* AND *YANG*.

As taught in texts books, *Yin* and *Yang* are explained in a simple way to enable the reader to obtain a 'feel' for their meaning in relation to each other and these explanations are important and useful, but in truth an attempt to reveal their wider values and meanings are expounded in the following Essays. It is important to understand that all and everything in existence is either *Yin* or *Yang* and/or a mix of both, engendering all the possible variation, complexity and diversification in life.

A glimpse, though shortened, at what the text books say:

YIN	YANG
Female	Male
Cold	Hot
Form	Force
Concrete	Abstract
Practice	Theory
Proof	Truth

These opposing terms are better understood as to their exquisite importance and true meaning within the pages of the following Essays:

WHAT EXACTLY IS THE CODE THAT ATTRACTS WOMAN (*YIN*) TO MAN (*YANG*) & WHY IS *YANG*/MALE EVENTUALLY REDEEMED BY *YIN*/FEMALE ?

THE CODE: The Heavenly Blueprint was to construct physical Male and physical Female within the mundane world but also with a Male and with a Female designation given to all phenomena - this would be the material reflection of this Heavenly but abstract/Ethereal-Plan or Blueprint.

This also meant the descent, wave after wave after wave of the components of this plan represented by ever more progressive densities of matter - the final product being the material Male and material Female presentation of what was originally conceived in Heaven - it was inevitable that the lower the descent, the more limiting and restricting the physical laws became/become, though still reflecting Heaven's **motive**.

Hence, the whole human-being is generated and completed, but everything not human is produced also, and is designated either Male or Female in **gender value**.

Even so, descent into matter of ever increasing density meant:

Built-in flaws in All and Everything; this is because we are all at a further distance, having descended, from the original blueprints of the perfection of Heaven, but and even so, The Process enables All and Everything to come into Being even with these deficiencies! Hence, as in Ayurvedic literature, man is born with a handicap as expressed in The *Doshas*. Also, as in the Talmud, it is stated that man is born with the evil impulse.

The material that made-up and makes-up these living Temporal Representatives would have to contain every possible element within the mundane plane: all possible metal/minerals, wood/fibre, water/fluids, fire/electricity, air/gasses/ether, and electromagnetic fields etc.,

The original Heavenly Spirit that animated and maintained life as it descended, would become less puissant as it birthed each lowered plane accompanied by its material elemental counterpart.

The stronger the Heavenly descending light, heat and spiritualistic motive, the more powerful and dense the material Earthly counterparts adhering to it.

So, the Heavenly Ethereal parts took-on physical attributes to **represent it** - *Yang*/Male (Heaven) had to become *Yin*/Female (Earth) to do just that. Therefore refined Heavenly abstractions became coarse Earthly matters. *Yang* had to become unrefined, even primitive, unsophisticated as well as harsh to allow itself to descend to each level. All phenomena both abstract and physical is a Heavenly and an Earthly representation that is Male and Female, both from the Blueprint conceived in Heaven as stated above.

All material things both animate and inanimate could be directly organised because they were now imbued with the fiery spirit of the fine energy/*Chi* of Heaven to enable order, ordinance and meaning to be an inseparable but penetrative aspect to them.

Therefore, for All and Everything else in existence as well. It meant that all Earthly mundane things and matter could now reflect its level of spirit/life by its organisation, regulation and formulation.

That is, the organisation and regulation that was already in Heaven but abstractly so, was now witnessed as a planned material reflect.

It meant also, that continual refinement of matter would bring this redeemed material closer to Home so to speak, that is, a way to return to Heaven where the source of everything began - this, to complete: The Cycle.

Further, that *Yin*/Female/Earth had/has the responsibility of refining material matters with All and Everything - She, *Yin*, takes the Male *Yang* fire within all things and is able with this *Yang* element to change matter from lead into gold, and also that of maintaining a calibrated account of All and Everything in existence.

Therefore She/*Yin* has to be attracted by a powerful interior compulsion to Male/*Yang* to undergo this task.

Did the descent of *Yang* contain within it the *Yin* material components already? That is, did all the material worlds come out of the *Yang*/Spirit/*Chi* descent, or were the material worlds of gas and dust already there, waiting for the spark of life, *Yang*/*Chi*, to give it purpose and meaning??? If dust and gas were already within the Universe of Space they would have to be freezing cold temperature-wise, and this Universe, filled with these particles of dust and gas, would have no physical Form as yet and also moribund absolute.

Yang could not do what it is meant to do when desiring to descend without material dust and gas already being present, acting as a medium to assist and to allow this *Yang* to condescend - is it the pull of opposites therefore that creates the first spark - gas and dust acting as a medium sufficient to ignite the first spark when *Yang* makes the first touch?

It is more likely that the gas and the dust material *Yin*, derived out and from Heaven simultaneously with the Yang spark, and/but had to explode to do so; that is **imploding** initially, before exploding, all within the first split second?!?!?!

On the final descent *Yang* became more *Yin*, that is, more materially inclined bit by progressive bit, and in this way, *Yin* became more *Yang* with this original *Yang* descent. It is a splendid mixture of both but only towards and within the physical realm.

Yin Female aspires to absorb and to appreciate the simpler uncomplicated 'straight lines' of Male *Yang*, and Male *Yang* aspires to absorb the more complicated rounded and curved lines of the Female *Yin*.

This process gives body to *Yang*, and innervates *Yin*. The so called Meridians, representing the visceral organs within the human body as of Chinese Medicine, and which influence a given organ, move in relatively straight lines but only because a given Meridian line of *Chi* energy is **spiral in its actual linear form,** in this case within the Meridian, but **minutely** so - a miniature elongated spring?

Even so and on the human level, why is the Female/*Yin* so engaged and attracted to the Male/*Yang*? She sees in the Male aspect of creation something that moves Her deeply at Her inner core.

This naturally affects her brain, heart and womb, so very basic, so foundational, so fundamental, so **fundament!** It is Her desire to help redeem Him; and the more Masculine He is, the more She needs to redeem and in this way be attracted to Him?

His descent from Heaven at first is ethereal and energetic and as He descends layer after layer He is taking on an Earthly body that should reveal to Him within and without how very basic He is now with his straight lines of form, with few curves, rough and ready and uncultivated so to speak. This is when Woman takes Him on; to help refine Him physically and culturally. She does this by embracing Him, absorbing Him, loving Him, caring for Him and rounding-off many of these sharp and primitive interior and exterior lines.

'........and with further definition:

If unredeemed, He is usually coarse in behaviour, generally hairier, boorish, unpolished, competitive, somewhat more physical than mental, rash, and with sharp rather than rounded contours both physically and psychologically and that is a known.

Even so, She needs his inherent abilities to activate, to warm-up, to disturb, and to excite Her.

Otherwise She may be inert, and potentially barren and cold! There has to be an initial chemical/physical attraction She has for Him, though ideally an attraction that is deep, fundamental and which moves Her very soul and bodily parts. (Read the very last Cameo at the very end of this book).

With this third force (Satva) of chemical attraction, subsequently She may now become attracted to his physique in addition to his protective tendencies and potential practical capabilities.

Further, why is She attracted to this unrefined physique and near troglodyte looks and the more brutal aspects of him in the first place?

It is that His soul energy is simple uncomplicated and therefore closer to Heaven - that may explain Her spiritual need to return to the uncomplicated source (Heaven). She being of Earth/*Yin* which creates the compulsion to re-attach and to rediscover Heaven/*Yang*:

The Source. (*Yang* attracts *Yin* and *Yin* attracts *Yang* all by irresistible compulsion). Just as two magnets will attract and hold each other firmly when the positive end of the one, pulls towards and attaches itself to the negative end of the other.

What about His physical attributes that attracts the Female? His physical attributes (Earth) reflect His spiritual origin that is in and from Heaven - He is Heaven but clothed now in all the materials of the mundane? For Him, She reminds Him from whence he originated. That is: Earth is Her origin but She has refined it - Her refinement and Her aspirations assist His return to Heaven.

That is: She is of Earth and that has to mean that Her Earthly attributes are a reflection of those ideas and attributes of numinous Heaven, and for Her, He reminds Her that She came into being from Earthly matter and has an Earthly practical role to fulfil.

His Earthliness that He has taken-on assists Her purpose on and in Earth, namely to breed and to refine mundane Earthly things.

The nature of his Earthliness, His interior chemistry must synchronise and resonate with Hers, then She will see and feel Him as Her own, and for Him to merge with Her and within Her.

She may execute all these things only with His input - She refines Earthly attributes and She civilises Him, for without Her input, He may tend to remain primitive in and on all levels without the desire to refine and redeem himself?

It is to be noted that, the positive effect of the feminine to help redeem him may not just be from the outside influence of a female human being, but from the influence of his deep feminine virtues within his own soul urging him on to purify and uplift his spiritual self!

WHY IS THERE A COMPELLING AND AN IRRESISTIBLE ATTRACTION BETWEEN MAN & WOMAN - PUT ANOTHER WAY: WHY IS THERE INSEPARABILITY BETWEEN *YIN & YANG?*

Man (Heaven-*Yang*) - Woman (Earth-*Yin*)

The key to the meaning of the contents of this Essay is to understand the significance of two complementary manifestations: Heaven/Male/Yang/Force/Energy and, Earth/Female/Yin/ Form/Matter. Note that there is some repetition here but with additional material on:

The Code:

These two sacred and super-great but paired emissaries of the Primum Mobile/Absolute are compelled to merge once again into each other as they were when they were originally conceived as such within the great Ethereal Omnipresence to enable creation in all its forms to manifest, but also because, once they have emerged from this diaphanous realm, that is, the moment they have been thrust out of the Absolute they are subject to the Laws of Mass from the finest to the densest. Their manifestations initially, are <u>sequential</u>, (read texts below), and being sequential rather than existing side by side as is the need and normal compulsion of opposites, a third-force is generated in the Universe - a fulcrum, a pivotal point, that acts as an adhesive of sorts; as an invisible gravitational pull; as a magnetic force that: Compels these opposites to cling each to the other once again, but especially so within the physical realm side by side. This is to compensate for the separation existing between the Male/Yang and the Female/Yin as a result of their <u>sequential</u> roles as depicted and embodied within the true meaning and purpose of the Chinese New Year. The Chinese New Year actually exists for the whole of humanity but Secularly. Everything in existence <u>persists</u> only because it is cosmically paired (Male & Female):

This third-force manifests out of the intense love and devotion and powerful desire for Male/ *Yang* and Female/*Yin* to cling each to the other as they were initially ONE in UNION within the Absolute/Primum Mobile. It may be stated that this third-force is: **LOVE**.

These opposites Male/*Yang* and Female/*Yin* whether in animal, vegetable or mineral also cling to each other as they do in object, and in subject under and above and at the sides of the Sun. The more pure and powerful these opposing forces, the stronger the attraction and the linkage!

These beloved emissaries, Male/*Yang* and Female/*Yin* exist to manifest Creation in all possible Forms. The Masculine emissary holds within him the essence of the Feminine - consequently the Feminine emissary may now manifest from her essence that which was latent within the Masculine. This Feminine emissary now realised, holds within her the essence of the Masculine, again to enable him, the Masculine to manifest again as an emissary. This new Masculine cycle has begun and holds within him again, the essence of the Feminine; and so: ad infinitum. Study the description of the Chinese New Year below:

Of The Chinese New Year, consider a sanctified ethereal and transcendental arm that has been thrust out of the Absolute or Primum Mobile whose purpose is to manifest all and everything within Creation.

Creation as we know it; and this is made possible by this sacred arm, whose energetic essence is Masculine/*Yang*/Heaven/Revelation in nature, descending, veering and unfolding as it develops, that begins to manifest <u>its</u> Female/*Yin*/Earth/Material aspect half way through its descent and development.

Thus, Creation may now manifest within this second phase from the half-way mark, approximately 180% in fact, this half-way mark represents the beginning of the **Formal** aspect of the Creation Cycle. Material Creation manifests via the Female/*Yin* input which now gives the original Masculine motive, which was abstract, the material FORM it requires to come into being, and does so via this Female/*Yin* second Phase/Cycle. The first half of the Chinese New Year is *Yang*/Male and the second half *Yin*/Female.

It is this second Phase/Cycle that is interesting. The *Yin*/Female force began around August/September and is developing in strength and manifestation reaching Her greatest power at around January/February of the following year.

Both Male and Female strength are about equal however, around October/November within this second phase of the Cycle that began August/September - it is therefore the best time to enjoy sexual-union for both Forces October/November ?!?!

It is also interesting that the Zodiacal Signs of Libra and Scorpio dominate this short period of October/November and each of these Signs amongst other things represent marriage and sexual-intercourse. This Third Force already mentioned has to be at its most powerful and is underscoring this short period of time.

This sacred thrusting Yang/*Male* arm unfolding does so circularly. When it reaches its zenith, which is at its greatest power, it does so, as in the texts above, at the approximate 180% mark. Then it begins a circular return journey but in its Female/*Yin* Form, and now physical manifestation

(*Yin*) may take place giving Form to the abstractions and ideas (*Yang*) of this Male Force. The Female/*Yin* Form reaches its zenith and greatest power at the Point of Renewal*

See the paragraph below. *Yang*/Male that began out of The Absolute January/February has transmogrified into *Yin*/Female at the point of the *Yang*/Male's extreme power of '*Chi*' at approximately 180%, its furthest point from whence it began, and in the time frame spanning 6 months approximately, towards the end of July and early August.

*The point of Renewal is where the Female/*Yin* energetic Cycle, that began approximately 6 months earlier, late August early September of the year before (Gregorian Calendar), reaches its zenith and its greatest power (January/February the following year). She then transmogrifies back into Male/*Yang* at the place where the *Yang*/Masculine cycle originally began (Renewal Point), which was/is at that place where the sacred arm **containing all that there is**, was thrust out of the Absolute; and at this point the Male/*Yang* Cycle will begin again January/February.

The '*Chi*' of the *Yin*/Female power at this zenith/Renewal point gives birth to *Yang*/Male, and these Cycles are thenceforth self-perpetuating but are so with **new character** (New Birth) - very different from the nature of the previous Cycle, **as was every cycle that had ever been and, will ever be.** See more on The Chinese New Year below. **This is a reality that is spiralling therefore, and not fixed circularly.**

Further, Female/*Yin* essence is already deep within the Male/*Yang*; analogous to the thrusting upwards of a plant, in the soil, driven by Male/Yang *Chi*; the *Chi* of creative energy or life, developing into the Form of a mature plant that takes-on the fibrous material and shape (Female/*Yin*) that represents the original archetypal abstract Plan (Male/*Yang*) but in material form (Female/*Yin*).

The genesis of the Female/*Yin* aspect that gives Form or material to the Theory, is held within the initial Male/*Yang* ethereal nature (conception and abstraction).

That is: at first the Plan and the Theory, becoming and developing into an object manifested, representing the Theory's mundane Form (Female/*Yin*). That which was originally conceived (Male/*Yang*) is now reflected materially (Female/*Yin*).

Just as one puts Theory into Practice. The first part is Male/*Yang* the second part is Female/*Yin*. Eve from Adam's rib is a useful metaphor here indeed!

As expounded above, it is the Sequential Cycle of The Chinese New Year, first Male, then Female, that underscores, that compels, that knowingly or unknowingly engineers the magnetic gravitational third force mentioned above within the first paragraph of this Essay, apart from the Absolute's purpose to Create, to compel the forces Male and Female to bind together i.e. Yin and Yang to cleave each to the other - this magnetic compulsion created is to initiate a side to side or coupling of partnership of Yin and Yang, Male and Female.

The sequential manifestation of Yang and then Yin is the quintessential aspect of the Chinese New Year. So now, there are two reasons why Yin clings to Yang and Yang to Yin - Male to Female - Heaven to Earth - Sun to Moon.

By the implication with the title of this Essay; its reference may now be understood as to the compelling and the gripping force, in the world of Mass from the finest to the densest, that pushes *Yin* and *Yang;* male and female onto, and into each other, including animal and vegetable - the passion and the desire to merge together and to be One, in Union; but this is also true for any object that is produced and for any subject propounded - proper manifestation of either means successful union of opposites *Yin/Yang;* Male/Female. Everything in existence persists because it is cosmically paired (Male/Female).

It is interesting to note that the Ancient Hindus, esoterically, named this third invisible but pivotal or gravitational force mentioned above as:

Sattvic (Sattva): The promise of something new but neutral, that impels and compels the forces of *Yin/Yang*, Male/Female, Heaven/ Earth to cleave to each other and thus, resolution is complete.

From a sacred and a cosmic point of view, the word for this compelling attraction would be:

'Love' omnipresent, that binds all and everything together.

Note: I repeat that this Male/Female concept may be difficult for us in the English Speaking World to understand, as our great language was neutered under the Saxon Kings about a thousand years ago. Objects and subjects were always given a male or a female gender rating; now devoid in our language but still extant in most other languages of the world.

According to esoteric lore, the essence that determines the male gender originates by exuding out of the ether or void (Absolute). This masculine ethos is likened to the primordial spirit, soul, and mind; whose sum-total engenders the focal point from which ideas are conceived. These ethereal attributes coalesce in Heaven (Absolute/*Yang*) and manifest within the male gender, **and because Heaven cleaves to Earth** this pre-programmed man, is compelled to attract to himself all Earthly attributes - he clothes himself in and absorbs Earthly mundane material; matters that are coarse and even mechanical. He is now in the thrall of Absolute/*Yin* and what was originally conceived is now in physical form representing the original idea.

These material aspects tend to dominate the male mind and heart, and according to the Old Testament, he is, that is, his body is indeed made-up of earthly flesh and blood/fluid.

The Hebrew name Adam (First Man) means Red/Earth. *Yang* Male ethereal *Chi* purity for the first half of the Cycle mentioned above, and for the second half of this Cycle the beginning of the material representation of that purity in all aspects as the Female/*Yin* Cycle gains strength, and gathers to it all mundane and temporal aspects of Creation.

Woman according to esoteric lore and whose interior ethos originates from out of the Temporal, Material and the Mundane, (second half of the Cosmic Cycle), possesses attributes of the heart and of the flesh but she is a more refined aspect of Earthly flesh (she being constructed from Adam's rib?) and, as such, the Female that is *Yin*/Earth, is compelled by the nature born of her interior being to find a way to back to merge with Heaven (attraction of opposites). It is the irresistible attraction to Heavenly things.

Therefore, being *Yin*/Earth she attracts to herself all the Heavenly attributes - she clothes herself in the more refined, ethereal, spiritual and matters hidden. Matters often unseen but applied nevertheless. Women, in the round, begin redeeming themselves almost automatically - Earth to Heaven:

The compelling and rigorous union!

The culminating point of this compulsion for her is at the point of Renewal as in the texts above, and she requires Male/*Yang Chi* to achieve this attribute from On High, whether by being impregnated with manly seed, and/or by being elevated transcendentally to the Heavenly Beatitude (The Convent).

For man to return to Heaven and Heavenly things - from whence his soul and nature of his mind and heart originally came - he has to experience and to suffer all that life presents and throws into his path.

With these life challenges, he has to work with rigour, has to struggle (Jacob struggling with an Angel. Tate Gallery London - Sculpture piece of Epstein), mostly employing induction, to win his redemption, and this, to enable his return to Heaven, (The Monastery), though this is optional for him! (At the point of Renewal he may move into reverse! The Prison or the Prison of Life). The return to Heaven's grace however, is possible only by deploying spiritual and altruistic work on himself, all to sublimate his basic and primitive instincts. Again, as it says in the Talmud: Man is born with the evil impulse - a product probably of the old brain that is the predatory reptilian part whose main component is the Cerebellum - perhaps more developed and therefore more primitive in its purposes in the male gender than in the female.

For woman - *Yin*/Earth attracted to *Yang*/Heaven - she is already on her way heavenwards by virtue of her captivation to higher and more loftier attributes as from the beginning, but also to the boundlessness of Heaven and Heavenly things.

In the male priesthood, it is the menfolk who are dominant in religious matters. Women in the round do not need the guidance and control that the menfolk require - his mind is virtually uncontrollable and certain 'canon laws' are required to curb his behaviour. Behaviour that is often unpredictable and dangerous. Meanwhile, he mistakenly thinks he is 'running the show'.

Women generally are more sensitive and cultivated and look Heavenwards anyway. The canon and secular laws have been brought into being by 'The Higher Unearthly Powers That Be' to give direction to man are needed less so for woman.

The male gender is capable of carrying-out the most terrible deeds supported by his guile and so he requires strict and rigorous control, though these are initially imposed on him from without, but following his self-realisation, (possible at the point of Renewal?) the requirement to change to loftier ways of being and living gainfully, should arise from within him!

This cosmic arrangement reveals women as generally stronger, and they may be able to endure more suffering as do menfolk - women instinctively know that the mundane life is temporary and the real journey is to return to the boundless heavenly source of all and everything, but also, it is the menfolk who require the religious restraints: they, being attracted to Earthly things - womenfolk need these restraints much less - they are already 'on the upward and return journey'.

In understanding the meaning of the texts above, it is well to see why men are attracted to women as they, men, originate ethereally from Heaven and compelled to absorb and enthuse worldly things as their spirit descends and especially to enjoy the Earthly and its sensual attributes - inherent gifts, we may assume from, and of, the voluptuous females' proclivities and attributes!

Then, what is it in women when originating out of the refined aspect of Earthly attributes, attracts them to the male gender. The male gender that originally descended from Heaven but had/has fallen, being obsessed by Earthly matters.

Since men have taken on an Earthly somewhat unrefined body compared to the female, whilst women have developed a more Heavenly gracious body of Earthly flesh, but elegant and and more cultivated, why is she attracted to the more coarse and the uncultivated?

Perhaps a woman when encountering the male gender is reminded of her Earthly origin and compelled by *Satva* to fulfil a duty, a promise, of realising the need to partake in a creative act and subsequently from out of her own flesh to create a newborn (again, at the point of Renewal - symbolically at least).

Also, unconsciously or consciously, to assist spiritually to help cultivate the male, to remind him from whence he originally came.

She perceives his original purity; his purity and simplicity before this purity became contaminated, contaminated by being immersed within the earthly passions - many of which are sinful. (Read 7 Deadly Sins later in this Book).

We do not need the Bible to tell us which of the earthly passions are sinful; we know them instinctively! The Seven Deadly Sins listed at the end pages of this book will assist comprehension of this point.

On a very basic level and on a practical note, most men would be happy living in squalor if not for the female requirement of improving mundane life by bringing hygiene and order round and about. After all, this is the first requirement for spiritual elevation which is, when manifested, for the male gender, to be abstemious and impeccable with the temporal and the foundational, leading to his Redemption journey-wise - The Monastic Approach!

However, another reason might be based on the fact that women generally perceive and are affected by the exudation of this Higher quality of energy of a given male individual before being beguiled by the physical way he looks:

The rarified Male *Yang* Heavenly Force dominates and will create an interior compulsion that engenders within him the need to integrate with and merge into the Female *Yin* Structure but only if the impression given by the Force of Her Body Type as well as her nature is harmonious and in-line with his particular Ethereal Heavenly *Chi*/Force, may that beautiful connection be made.

To be in harmony implies alignment of this ethereal force from him with the force of her receptivity. In terms of science, both magnetic and electrical fields exuding from them both tend to dove-tail and are therefore consonant and business may be conducted, so to speak!

This complementary connection has now created a Third Force. This Third Force is *Satvic (Satva)* as taught by Hindu esoteric knowledge of the *Gunas* and implies the employment of a fulcrum, that is, a point neither male nor female, generated through the alignment of this splendid mutual connection of male and female.

This *Satvic* fulcrum may be thought of as **conditional** love that results from the binding of the male and the female together in union. *Satva* comes into being when there is alignment and subsequent harmony between these two gender forces, but only because of this immensely powerful attracting element.

In different words, the mundane Earthly elements have to be receptive for that particular Heavenly *Chi* to manifest itself within it, and thus that mundane material element has now come alive because it been imbued with Heavenly *Chi*. The temporal and the material of the mundane is essential to Him, but for Her the quality and type of energy or *Chi* from Him matters first before the physical attraction.

Applied to woman, she is more impressed by his behaviour mental and emotional initially before his physical type is considered. Applied to man, he is taken by the look and body shape of the female first, the mental/emotional aspects come later.

It may be deduced from the very difficult to comprehend texts above that, the desire within the absolute/primum mobile to manifest its heavenly male attributes into the temporal world of mass by manufacturing physicality which is that realm of the feminine attribute, <u>he</u> (upstairs) was No Doubt urged-on to do his coming-out as expounded above by <u>his</u> female side of <u>his</u> ethereal nature - <u>she</u> insisting on becoming known to enable life in all its complexity and diversity to Manifest into being on Earth!

Therefore, when we pray, and recite The Lord's Prayer, perhaps We should address it thus: our father <u>and mother</u> which art in heaven. Rather than: our father which art in heaven !?!?!? In life, after all, it is the women who subtly lead the menfolk....whether we THE MENFOLK like it or not !

Chinese Proverb: Man sees the bigger picture (centrifugation) woman sees the detail (centripetal-isation)!

ADDENDUM

DISCLOSING THE UNIVERSAL CODE FROM
IDEA TO FORMATION
(Part 2)

**From hereon-in, further material on THE CODE is expounded with
inevitable repetition but with additional material, that includes
Astrological references from both the Chinese and the European.**

*At first there is the idea, the conception, following this, the planning takes place, then the physical
form is developed that eventually reflects the glory of that original idea. That idea once diaphanous
is now manifest within the physical reality in which we live. To offer a simple example: A certain
type of chair for a particular purpose is in the mind of the artisan. Technically, he then sketches
his idea on paper or by engaging the facilities of a computer. Once certain decisions have been
made as to the materials to be employed, he proceeds to construct that chair from the original
plans that were in his mind and from the material he has chosen, and now that initial idea has
become a physical form - a chair. Actually, this procedure explains is a perfect Algorithm.*

*Above: The conception is Yang/Masculine and the eventual physical reflection of that
conception is Yin/Feminine. Binary Code: Zero is Yang/Male and One is Yin/Female.*

FURTHER: AS WITH ALL SUBJECTS & OBJECTS UNDER THE SUN; THESE ARE THE MATERIAL
REFLECTIONS OF ETHEREAL CONSTITUENTS OF THE ABSOLUTE - THE ABSOLUTE THAT IS
BOUNDLESS AND WHICH CONFOUNDS AND CONFUSES AND IS THE THEORETICAL SOURCE
OF ALL & EVERYTHING TO WHICH WE HUMAN BEINGS MAY HAVE OCCASIONAL ACCESS.

LET US TAKE HOMO SAPIENS AS ONE OF THESE SUBJECTS: HIDDEN ELEMENTS WITHIN
MAN ENGENDER AN IRRESISTIBLE ATTRACTION TO HIS FEMALE CONSORT, AND APART
FROM THESE ELEMENTS/FORCES INCITING WITHIN HIM THE PROPENSITY TO PRODUCE
PROGENY: WHY? PUT ANOTHER WAY: WHY IS THERE COMPULSIVE INSEPARABILITY
BETWEEN YIN/FEMALE & YANG/MALE?

Man (Heaven-*Yang*) - Woman (Earth-*Yin*)

NOTE: as mentioned earlier in the texts of some of these essays, this Male/Female concept may be difficult for us English Speaking People to understand, as our splendid but mongrel language was neutered by design or by accident, under the Saxon Kings between 900 and 1300 A.D.

Nouns and adjectives were always given a Male and a Female gender rating before 900AD in old English, now devoid in modern-day English but still extant [gender rating] in most other languages of the world. The consequences of this, what some might call a defect, has caused in the English Speaking Generations since, and especially up to the present day, the inability to appreciate the exquisite differences and nuances of Male and Female nomenclature in all and everything. Which might explain our boorish attitudes in so many departments of life!?!?!?

To convey to the reader a better understanding of the nature of these Essays: The Chinese New Year may be employed, as its hidden meaning and purpose should offer the key to unlock the intricacies of the following texts.

Indeed, the CNY is an analogue for the purpose of *YIN* & *YANG*. In addition, the meanings of many of the texts are repeated several times though in slightly different ways to enable the grasping of the meaning of the essence of this particular expounding.

THE CHINESE NEW YEAR (CNY) FROM THE MORE ESOTERIC VIEWPOINT:

Of The Chinese New Year, end of January/early February on any given year, consider a sanctified ethereal and transcendental arm that has been thrust out of the Absolute or Primum Mobile whose purpose is to manifest all and everything within Creation - Creation as we know it.

This is made possible by this sacred arm, whose energetic essence is Masculine/*Yang*/Heaven/Revelation and therefore diaphanous in nature, descending, veering and unfolding as it develops, that begins to manifest <u>its</u> Female/*Yin*/Earth/Material and therefore temporal aspect as from its half-way Mark from July/August of that year.

Yang/Heaven/Masculine: His nature is to supply the original ideas and the inspiration but also the Revelation to enable She, the Feminine/*Yin* to create the Form in, and to which these abstract matters may come into being.

Therefore, Creation in all its forms, that is: His output, may only manifest with Her practical input. It is all a wondrous Cycle.

In the first half of a Cycle of creation, *Yang*/Masculine issues forth *Truth* but Truth only in theory, and in the second half of this Cycle, the Female/*Yin* aspect demands physical, concrete *Proof* of that *Truth!* Analogous to the true meaning of The Chinese New Year in that the first half (*Yang*) manifests <u>potential</u> creative glory and the second half (*Yin*) actuates this glory into our reality. This glorious Cycle works within us and all living things - it is life-inseparable.

Woman (Earth/*Yin*): Her nature is to resolve, slow-down, restrain and engender material things, applying centripetal force/friction consciously or unconsciously.

What are produced in this way are the products of the Temporal. Temporal matters become refined and precious in value and from these developments, She is able to bring into being, at Her <u>finale</u> a new *Yang*/Masculine Cycle.

THE HALF-WAY MARK OF THE CNY

The half-way mark referred to above of The Chinese New Year is approximately 180% distance from its genesis.

The *Yang*/Male abstract inspiration and aspiration, moving through its descent is nearing full development, though His attributes are still theoretical in nature as He reaches this 180% Mark; but now the second phase out of this arena may truly begin.

Indeed, following July/August of that year, there is the realisation of an inkling of materiality that reflects in a physical way the earlier Male/*Yang* inspirations and aspirations as the *Yin*/Feminine temporal phase takes-hold. This taking-hold gathers strength and solidity until late January/early February of the following year. At Her maximum mortal strength, dissipation and dissolution is now apparent at the point of Renewal, and at the point of Renewal a New Year begins (See below).

THE EXTRAORDINARY SPIRALLING POINT OF RENEWAL

The Point of Renewal is where the Female/*Yin* energetic Cycle has reached its zenith and its greatest power of solidity and gravity. These attributes began approximately 6 months earlier, late August/early September of the year before (Gregorian Calendar).

She has now transmogrified, at the Point of Renewal, back into Male/*Yang* at the place where the *Yang*/Masculine cycle originally began (Renewal Point), which was/is at that place where the sacred arm **containing all that there is,** was thrust out of the Absolute; and at this point the Male/*Yang* Cycle will begin again January/February born out of the *Yin*/Feminine.

The Essence of the *Yin*/Female power at this zenith (Renewal point) gives birth to *Yang*/Male as explained above, and these Cycles are henceforth self-perpetuating but are so with <u>new character</u> (New Birth) - very different from the nature of the previous Cycle, as was every cycle that <u>had</u> ever been and, <u>will</u> ever be. This is a reality that is <u>spiralling</u> therefore, and not fixed <u>circularly</u>.

In a more detailed way: The *Yang*/Masculine force descends from Heaven (The Absolute) and initially burgeoning in essence. He is feeding off the material elements that are nourishing his growth and his strength supplied by the *Yin*/Feminine aspect of creation of the previous Cycle (just as woman supports man). In time as He descends and expands, He is irresistibly gaining control in His descent, with his power, strength, heat, light, *chi*, movement and dominance. However, the *Yin*/Female spirit is hidden within Him ready to manifest at the right phase of time in this new Cycle.

The *Yang*/Male puissance is in the form of His intellectual resources, ideas and creativity, and interestingly, the whole picture described is one of abundant energy with velocity that is centrifugal in nature; that is:

Spreading and expanding in its influence; ethereal and abstract to begin with but is now becoming more concrete and is beginning to take multiple physical forms because Her influence is present as the cusp is reached representing the change in the Creation Cycle in question, when Her power of bringing-in practicalities commences and His ethereal influences wane.

The inflationary process of creative ideas, once complete, becomes weakened as the more practical elements of creation take place at the 180% junction reflecting these abstractions but in the way of the more physical. Thus, what is now engendered is the *Yin*/Earth/Feminine force (His Consort) manifests materiality though without great power at this initial stage.

Yin is Earth/Feminine, and She is concerned with physicality in essence as explained above. She is irresistibly drawn upwards and inwards in an Ascent, becoming more powerful as She does so, coalescing and concentrating Her multiple practical possibilities.

Indeed, these temporal matters are refined as She will be at Her most forcefulness, but She is also carrying hidden with Her the spirit of *Yang*/Masculine.

He has invigorated Her throughout Her dominant second half of the Cycle via the power of the first *Yang*/Masculine half that still has its influence, though of course to a much lesser degree. **Even so, *Yang* is more focused within *Yin* as *Yang* now has purpose and practical function**.

At the advanced stage, towards the Point of Renewal, She is consolidating, cooling and objective. She is at her greatest strength and now all these attributes crystallise into multiple Forms. Then the process of dis-integration begins. Thus, She may now give way or give birth to *Yang*/Masculine/Heaven - clearing the way for a new Cycle at the Point of Renewal.

THE PARADOX - YANG REPLACES YIN AND YIN REPLACES YANG

The meanings of the texts above may seem to be in contradiction when, let us say, lovely fragrant flowers are looked upon and experienced by the senses, compared to harsher forms of matter as in the coarse materials of a building whether aesthetically pleasing or not, in that the flowers are thought to be Feminine and the building to be Masculine. The more concentrated forms, as explained above are Feminine (the building) and the more delicate ethereal forms are Masculine (the flower).

Yet it has to be remembered that it is the *Yang*/Male energy of the ethereal life force that animates the plant within the soil that ultimately generates the flower - it is the *Yin*/Female energy of consolidation that creates the physical form of the plant out of which the flower arises.

As might be understood now, how with compulsion, *Yang* attaches itself to *Yin* and *Yin* attaches itself with compulsion to *Yang*.

Michio Kushi (Macrobiotics) points out that a woman has her strength and power concentrated interiorly - Her *Yang* rarefied energy within the inside of her attracts the *Yin* heavier structure within the inside of her and she is weaker exteriorly. Whilst that of a man, he has his strength and his power exteriorly - His *Yang* rarefied energy on the outside creates *Yin* heavier structure on the outside and thus he is weaker interiorly.

Women could not undergo **gravidation** if they were devoid of the power and endurance of strong physicality interiorly, and menfolk could not undertake most of the physical and arduous tasks needed to be carried-out in life without being externally hardy and robust to enable these external labours to be undertaken.

MAN: He is naturally *Yang* and this powerfully attracts *Yin* (centripetal) and so he is strongly built on the outside .
WOMAN: She is naturally *Yin* and this powerfully attracts *Yang* (centrifugal) and so she is built softly on the outside
MAN: His outside *Yin chi* energetics being centripetal/concentrated engenders strong physical characteristics.
WOMAN: Her outside *Yang chi* energetics being centrifugal/dispersed engenders soft feminine characteristics.

Quote: Dame Rebecca West: There is, of course, no reason for the existence of the male sex except that sometimes one needs help with moving the piano.

An additional key to the understanding of the meaning of the contents of this Essay, and the texts above, is to comprehend the significance of the two complementary presentations: Heaven/Male/Yang/Force/Energy - which engenders movement away from the centre, that is centrifugation and, Earth/Female/Yin/Form/Matter - which engenders movement towards the centre, coalescing centripetally, but in actual practice, Heaven's Yang Force tends to move downwards and outwards towards Earth, and with Earth's Yin Force, movement tends to be upwards and inwards towards Heaven. This explains better the structure of The Chinese New Year - it's first half descends and it's second half ascends. For simplicity, I will continue to use YANG for Man/Heaven and YIN for Woman/Earth and without italics. Also the meanings of the contents of this Essay will become clearer as the reader proceeds through the texts below. There is a certain amount of repetition. Again, I have to warn the reader because a few of these Essays were re-written in different periods.

THE PRIMUM MOBILE - THE ABSOLUTE

Within the <u>invisible</u> etheric world of The Primum-Mobile - The Absolute, where there is all that there is, and that includes the YANG and the YIN attributes of the Universe, it is the YANG attribute at its genesis, that is thrust-out of His diaphanous realm of the The Primum-Mobile and as He descends, so are the visible worlds and visible world created but mainly in conception at this juncture with accompanying Work in Progress.

Yet it was the YIN aspect within the <u>invisible</u> etheric of the Primum-Mobile (Absolute), that was the motive force that initiated the thrusting-out of Her YANG partner to descend and expand creatively, and in this way, both the YIN and the YANG (Female & Male) could reflect the grandeur of The Absolute/Primum-Mobile, but now in Material/Temporal Form because:

The YIN aspect of creation within The Absolute, that originally caused the YANG to be thrust-out and be revealed, may only manifest through the YANG aspect that descends and expands. In other words, YANG/He, carried the She/YIN seed which sprouted as it descended and began its earthly existence only when He/YANG had fully exhausted His potential through intensive expansion of His Ideas and His Radiance. Altogether, YIN and YANG needed to reflect themselves in physical form by Earthly means.

Again, the meanings of all these statements become clearer under the following texts:
IT MAY BE STATED THAT: IT IS THE CREATOR (Male & Female) WITHIN
THE PRIMUM MOBILE (Indeed is The Primum Mobile) DESIRING TO KNOW
ITSELF IN EARTHLY FORM AND EMPLOYS BOTH HEAVEN AND EARTH
AS THE TOOLS BY WHICH THIS KNOWING MAY TAKE PLACE!

Further: This descent of Male/YANG, at first ethereal and nebulous is carrying with Him, apart from His creative ideas, revelations and inventions, the Essence of all that is embodied within the Feminine/YIN seed. That is: the Feminine/YIN germ, that must eventually give birth to existence.

YANG *chi* becomes hotter, brighter, intelligent and **focused** because it has **YIN Form** to channel it **articulately and thus Yang is refined.** However, in time it suffers energy loss, as gravity and solidity begin to dominate. There is transmogrification at this juncture into the full Feminine/YIN aspect of creation. Thus, She begins to dominate the frame with Her temporal dictates.

YIN that is actually the beginning of physical creation and terrestrial at Her genesis, begins ascending very slowly and heavily carrying with it the Essence of YANG, and has begun a return journey in time, step by step. As She progresses, She becomes more ethereally inclined, and so materiality is now Heavenly and radiant in content because the YANG spirit is able to shine deploying Her material nature through which [it] Yang may actualise in full refinement. (Look once again at the beautiful lattice-work of dressed-stone that adorns the Great Cathedrals and other great buildings of significance - you are witnessing refined material YANG within YIN). Then eventually She evolves into Male YANG once again at The Point Of Renewal*.

SEQUENTIAL ROLES OF YIN & YANG

*At this extreme point of 'Change Over', perhaps some kind of ignition takes place and a spark of sorts appears from out of this mass. The spark is YANG. YANG manifesting initially, followed by burgeoning YIN may now be seen as <u>sequential</u> in realisation. YIN and YANG do not emerge simultaneously from the Absolute or from [Heaven]. At the beginning, Yang alone emerges, but containing the Yin seed....

Even so, these two sacred and super-great but paired emissaries YIN & YANG of the Primum Mobile/Absolute are compelled to merge once again into each other as they were when they were originally conceived as such within the great Omnipresence to enable creation in all its forms to be visible and tangible, but also because, once Yang has emerged from His translucent realm, that is, the moment He has been thrust out of the Absolute He is subject to the laws of Mass (Feminine).

He carries within Him the Yin Essence of creation, that He is programmed to manifest at a given moment of time. Yin and Yang reveal themselves sequentially, as stated above, rather than side by side, as is the need and normal compulsion of opposites, and so a third-force is generated in the universe.

This is a fulcrum, a pivotal point, that acts as an adhesive of sorts; as an invisible gravitational pull; as a magnetic force that: Compels these opposites to cling each to the other once again.

THE UNBEARABLE SEPARATION OF YIN & YANG

To compensate for the separation existing between the Male/Yang and the Female/Yin as a result of their <u>sequential</u> roles as depicted above in the texts and embodied within the Chinese New Year, this third-force mentioned above, is spontaneously issued from out of the intense love and devotion and powerful desire of Male/Yang and Female/Yin to cling each to the other as they were initially as ONE in UNION within the Absolute/Primum Mobile.

From the esoteric point of view, the inner meaning of The Chinese New Year happens to attest to much more than its normal purpose and function. Everything in existence <u>persists</u> only because it is cosmically paired! As stated earlier, this glorious Cycle is inside us and in all living things.

These opposites Male/Yang and Female/Yin whether in animal, vegetable or mineral also cling to each other as they do in object, and in subject under and above and at the sides of the Sun. The more pure and powerful these opposing forces, the stronger the attraction and the linkage! Again: Everything in existence <u>persists</u> only because it is cosmically paired.

These beloved emissaries, Male/Yang and Female/Yin exist to manifest Creation in all possible Forms. Again, the Masculine emissary holds within him the essence of the Feminine - consequently this Feminine emissary may now bring into being from her essence, her attributes - her attributes that were latent within the Masculine emissary.

Further, this Feminine emissary now realised, holds within her the essence of the Masculine, again to enable him, the Masculine emissary to manifest again at the right moment of time (The Renewal Point). This new Masculine cycle to be, holds within him again, the essence of the Feminine; and so on: ad infinitum.

Again, it is as well to mention here that the YANG described above as moving away from its centre as it is centrifugal in nature, but downwards in motion to re-unify with YIN.

He is impatient to bond again with YIN yet to manifest - the YIN, that has Her essence within him. In the same way Her eagerness is to re-construct Herself centripetally and then to move upwards, because She is impatient to re-bond again with Him (YANG), and in this way be energised again by Him (YANG). This obsessive tendency therefore causes them to chase each other around but in circles as couples do!

Perhaps the only time they do catch-up with each other is when intercourse/congress takes place twice yearly! - she being dominant end of summer, and he being dominant end of winter. Read again the description of the Chinese New Year above, from page 77 onwards.

'........and put another way: Material Creation manifests because of the Female/Yin input, which now gives the original Masculine motive, that was abstract, the physical FORM it requires for it to come into being; and does so via this Female/Yin second Phase/Cycle.

As already stated, the first half of the Chinese New Year is Yang/Male and the second half Yin/Female. Even so, it may be argued that the Yang phase is already present in that first half of the CNY as is the Yin phase already present in the second half of the Chinese New Year.

It is the moving tide of energy starting at The Renewal Point, that galvanises these two phases at the appropriate times?

Again, this sacred thrusting-out of the Yang/Male arm unfolding does so circularly. When it reaches its zenith, which is at its greatest power, it does so, as described in the texts above, at the approximate 180% Mark. Then it begins a circular return journey but in its Female/Yin Form, and now absolute physicality and refinement may take place, (as with beautiful antique furniture adorned with gold filigree and more). This Female/Yin Form reaches its zenith and greatest power of dismantlement at the Point of Renewal.

Yang/Male that began out of The Absolute January/February has been fully transmogrified into Yin/Female at the point of the Yang/Male's greatest realisation at approximately 180%, its furthest point from whence it began, and in the time frame spanning 6 months approximately, towards the end of July and early August.

Female/Yin essence is already deep within the Male/Yang; analogous to the thrusting upwards of a plant driven by Male/Yang *Chi*; the *Chi* of creative energy or life, developing into the Form of a mature plant, from the soil that takes-on the fibrous material and shape (a synthesis of Male/

Yang & Female/Yin) that represents the original **archetypal** life force or abstract Plan (Male/Yang) but with **constituents/components** (Female/Yin).

The genesis of this Female/Yin aspect that promotes the giving of Form or Substance to the theoretical plan, is held within the initial Male/Yang ethereal nature (conception and abstraction). That is: at first the Plan and the Theory, becoming and developing into an object manifested, representing the Theory's Form (Female/Yin). That which was originally conceived is now reflected in Matter.

JUST AS ONE PUTS THEORY INTO PRACTICE. THE FIRST PART IS MALE/YANG THE SECOND PART IS FEMALE/YIN. EVE FROM ADAM'S RIB COULD BE A USEFUL METAPHOR INDEED! EVEN SO, IT WAS THE FEMININE WITHIN ADAM THAT MOTIVATED THIS ACTION THAT HAD THESE AMAZING CONSEQUENCES!

As expounded above, it is the Sequential Cycle, as revealed by The Chinese New Year, first Male, then Female, that underscores, that compels, that knowingly or unknowingly becomes the prime-mover for this magnetic third force to do its work. This is in addition to the Absolute's purpose to Create, which virtually forces Male and Female to be bound together i.e. Yin and Yang to cleave each to each other.

However, this magnetic third force of compulsion generated is to compel the Masculine and the Feminine to try to exist side by side in all and everything and not just sequentially as one entity following the other - sequentially as elucidated within the inner meaning of Chinese New Year. So, there are two reasons, two different urges that causes Yin to cling to Yang and Yang to cling to Yin - Male to Female - Heaven to Earth and the esoteric meaning of the inseparability of the Sun (masculine) and of the Moon (feminine).

By the implication of the title of this essay; its meaning may now be understood as: The compelling and the gripping force, in the world of Mass, that pushes yin and yang; male and female onto, and into each other, including animal and vegetable - the passion and the desire to merge together and to be One, in Union; but this is also true for any object that is produced and for any subject propounded - proper manifestation of either means successful union of opposites yin/yang; male/female. Everything that exists is PAIRED. As stated above: Everything in existence persists only because it is paired. To mend something we say: repair it!

THE SATVIC THIRD FORCE

It is interesting to note that the Ancient Hindus, esoterically, named this third invisible but pivotal or gravitational force as in the texts above: Sattvic (Sattva): The promise of something new, but neutral to both forces, that impels and compels the Yin/Yang, Male/Female, Heaven/Earth to cleave to each other and thus, resolution should prevail.

From a sacred and a cosmic point of view, the word for this compelling attraction could be:

LOVE omnipresent, that binds all and everything together.

This Satvic fulcrum may be thought of as **conditional LOVE** that results from the binding of the Male and the Female together in Union. Satva comes into being when there is alignment and subsequent harmony between these two gender forces, but only because of this powerful attracting element.

See Earlier Essay: Why Is There a Compelling & An Irresistible Attraction Between Man & Woman page. The essence of this Essay has been distilled, amongst other elements, from the essential purpose, meaning and hidden function of the Chinese New Year - its Male/Yang and its Female/Yin aspects.

THE CHINESE NEW YEAR PART TWO

IN THE OPINION OF THE AUTHOR THE CNY IS THE TRUE BUT <u>SECULAR NEW YEAR FOR HUMANITY</u> AS A WHOLE FOR THE FOLLOWING REASONS:

Applying <u>Ptolemaic</u> Astrology, CNY begins either towards the end of January or early to mid February - its year on year variation accords to the position of the Moon in relation to the Sun (New Moon). In fact it is always begins with a conjunction of both Lights (Sun & Moon) in the Zodiacal Sign of Aquarius (In European Astrology). Immediately following and after which the character and colour of the year is determined such as with its Animal representation and importantly the (Chinese) <u>Element</u> of that New Year that gives expression to it, that is: the type of energetic quality in the air, so to speak, that will determine the ethos of 'That Time', be it the fashion of 'That Time' and the mood of humanity at 'That Time'.

In addition, the Planets and their angular relationships to this New Moon on that day have a profound effect on this New Year and for the whole of its 12 months and which has a serious and far-reaching effect on, and in, all of humanity and probably all living creatures as well as, for example the abundance and the quality of vegetation.

THE CHINESE NEW YEAR EXTRAORDINAIRE OF 2011

Taking The Chinese New Year of 2011 for instance; this New Year came into being at the point when the Sun and the Moon were conjunct at 14 degrees approximately within the Sign of Aquarius, but also Planet Mars coincidentally happened to be at that same degree of the same Sign within minutes.

It could therefore be predicated that War should break-out that year violently and relentlessly and would probably remain unresolved for several years being such a powerful configuration.

In fact the so-called Arab Spring* began then and has not ended to date - spilling-over into other New Years. The consequences of which are frightening to countenance. New Years affect both the personal the business and the political scenes the world over and more.

POLITICS

* A Western World term coined in ignorance at the time, and later much regretted - stupid and naive Western minds thinking that a mutable blooded people could rule themselves under a democratic system, a system that took a thousand years plus to develop for us Europeans and the Arab and Muslim peoples' could do it in 5 minutes! The democratic system only just about works for us Europeans! (Keep Brexit in mind).

It may also be stated that the 2011 Chinese New Year was a Metal Element and a Animal Rabbit Year. Meaning, that the Planet Venus, ruler of Metal in Chinese lore, and planet Jupiter ruler of the Rabbit Mode, would have its affect positively and negatively, such as to cause in worldly terms:

At worst: boundless optimism and conviction about the way certain things should be undertaken and the consequent disasters when these ways of doing things go wrong; mainly from misjudgment and the inability to discriminate. At best: to see the excellence and the positivity in things and <u>conserving</u> those subjects and objects that work well and are proven.

'........but there would be (Venus) competitiveness - almost every person, institution, government, party and firm would be vying for their '15 minutes of fame' and short-term fortune. In addition, many individuals would try, misguidedly, to weaken Authority by trying to expand the power of (Jupiter) democracy that is somewhat lame now, in all the spheres of life employing so called **equality** as the tool with which to weaken even more essential rulership and leadership. Consequently, the great conundrum presented, that is, the consequences of this sort of 'mission creep' has caused, and is causing: Disruption in the world leading to the potential destruction of our Political Systems - this is the regrettable result of the present-day attitude that is prevalent amongst the demos, an attitude that expresses the terrifying and liberal notion:

That 'Anything Goes', And That There Should Be A Further Diminution Of All That Is Sacred And All That Has Been Proven Over Millenia.

Confidentially, this secular and liberal notion - that 'anything goes' - happens to be repulsive, unbearable and anathema to Islam in particular, but it is also in this way with Christianity and with Judaism but to a lesser obsessive degree.

AN UNHAPPY PLANET EARTH

Is it any wonder we have a very troubled planet. Not that the planet is ever not troubled, but in this horrifying epoch, extremely so. Many thinking people would agree that a democracy 'gone mad', such ours, weakens authority and therefore government. It is a dangerous defect in our governmental way of life, because we have become feeble in our use of words and in our actions as sentimentality has been and is being mistaken for compassion. We are disallowed to 'call a spade a spade' and we are are less aware of certain very important realities in the present epoch - such as with the disgusting behaviour of many of us human-beings; behaviour not so much of the ruling classes as we tend to blame, but of the demos, the people, that considers itself above reproach!

THE FIVE GREAT ELEMENTS TO WHICH WE ARE SUBJECT

There are 5 great Elements (Chinese). Each of these is ruled by a Planet; a Planet that drives the energy of that Element which in turn also powers that particular Yearly Cycle in question and to a large extent gives that Cycle its character for that year.

Jupiter propels <u>Wood</u>; Mars propels <u>Fire</u>; Saturn propels <u>Earth</u>; Venus propels <u>Metal</u>; Mercury propels <u>Water</u>.

The Chinese New Year begins heralding an archetypal Element (Chinese) and as such it is always different to the Element of the Year before. In addition, a new Animal character enters the scene different from the one belonging to the Year before. The Chinese Five Elements underlined above are: Wood, Fire, Earth, Metal, and Water - in that order.

The Wood Element per se underscores the Chinese New Year at its beginning regardless of the new and changing Elements of each year. In other words, it subsumes all the other Elements. The Wood Element has many cosmic functions within Creation. One in particular is that it holds the unrelenting power to initiate things; that is: engendering phenomena.

Indeed from the Chinese Medicine point of view and within man, his Gall Bladder*, driven by the Wood Element, compels him both psychologically and emotionally to get him off his backside to begin work, recreation, enterprise and whatever kind of activity in life all requiring <u>decisive</u> action.

It is the same coercive energy that primes the starting point of the Chinese New Year. The only difference is that the scale is universal rather than personal. The visceral organ ruled by the Aquarian Sign is the Gall Bladder.

The visceral organs of the body also generate particular emotional and mental phenomena and not just their known physiological functions.

THE PTOLEMAIC SIGNS OF THE HEAVENLY ZODIAC

The new Yang Cycle (Yang/Masculine) has begun at the Renewal point, as explained in earlier chapters, and is the point, in fact that heralds the Chinese New Year.

It passes through an evolutionary process of development via the Signs of the Zodiac (from Aquarius to Pisces to Aries to Taurus to Gemini to Cancer) gaining strength and purpose and reaching its greatest magnetic strength, its zenith, in late July or early August.

Early August witnesses the period termed: The Great Heat. (Northern Hemisphere) Then, at this time, out of Yang/Masculine, the Feminine/Yin aspect the so-called Fall begins (late August, September and October). These months represent the period of the coming together of matters Temporal.

This Yin/Feminine aspect increases its strength, but refined creative strength, through the latter Zodiacal Signs from Scorpio onwards through to Sagittarius and then to Capricorn all over a 3 month period - She then manifests fully Her Earthly<u> objective in all creative ways. (Such as with beautiful furnishings and fabrics as well as dressed stone - this is on a more physical level, but on a more ethereal level: refined and spiritual behaviour - **redemption).**</u> This Yin/Feminine zenith around the January/February time of the following year and which is called: The Great Cold, is at the period of The Renewal Point within the Sign that follows Capricorn, and that is: the Zodiacal Sign Aquarius, and as expressed above heralds the CNY, from which the New Year Yang/Masculine Cycle has and will emerge.

The Yearly Cycles, as already explained, enjoy a new Element with each succession and as such, that new Element colours the Wood Foundation Element that underlies it, but to be precise, and as the Elements are made-up of Male/Yang and Female/Yin, we witness a 2 year period that covers the same Element but with the 1st year of the two, stamped as Yang Male and the 2nd year of the two, stamped as Yin Female.

This totals-up to a 10 year period cycle that gives a 2 year ownership to each of the Five Elements, but with the first year Male/Yang and the second year Female/Yin.

A MONKEY YEAR

Taking an example: 1944 was a **Monkey Year** and simultaneously Wood Element - 60 years later 2004 the exact same configuration took place:

Taking the number 60 further: If enlightened by seeing this 'Bigger Picture' and also having the capacity to speculate, it could be proffered that man's lease of life might be 120 years. The first 60 being Yang and the second 60 being Yin. The first 60 learning skills and active in all capacities (Yang), and the second 60 passive dissemination of knowledge and the conveyance of wisdom - Yin attributes. Knowledge and wisdom should be gained by the rigours of the first 60 years of life.

At around the age of 60, usually, a person is at the height of his/her powers in knowledge and possesses a sort of 'knowing' but is also, usually, materially at his/her peak. The enjoyment of possessing material means with attendant good sense bodes well for the enjoyment of the following 60 years, which engages the wisdom and capacity for mentoring others but derived from the activities of the first 60 years of a given life.

As with The Chinese New Year, its first half presenting activity (Yang), and its second half presenting consolidation (Yin), then a full life as mentioned in the previous paragraph, but applying a smaller scale the same pattern is held, in let us say, a life of 90 years (which is becoming the norm more so in the Western World), probably has the first 45 as: the learning with rigour and the second 45 as enjoying the rewards of the disciplines of the first 45 year tranche by giving constructive advice and mentoring in the latter. Only the scale is different in that the pattern of a given year with its two halves represents on a smaller scale a full life of say 90 years with its two halves of 45.

Taking this further: Those who see life evolving over billions of years as advocated by the scientific method, may now understand that symbolically and biblically:

Seven days to bring heaven and earth into being may be understood if we ratio 0.64 billion years to one-day. That gives us approx 4.5 billion years (approximate age of the Earth) to 7 biblical days. Think of this ratio conversion as SYMBOLIC.

The first 2.2 billion years or 3 and a half days may be given to conception in the form of gases and elementals (Yang) and the second 2.2 billion years or 3 and a half days given as consolidation and structuring of the Earth (Yin) to support life as we know it. (All billions stated are approximate values

Five Seasons or Elements (Chinese) are awakened within each Yearly Cycle as well. Wood to Fire to Earth to Metal to Water and Water return to Wood. Each of these Elements endure for approximately two and a quarter months give or take. Totalling the number of the twelve month Cycle.

THE INSEPARABILITY OF THE SOLAR SYSTEM AND THE EARTH (THEY ARE ALL ASPECTS OF ONE MODULE)

As regards to our Solar Planetary System, which is mirrored within us Homo Sapiens as well as in all forms of life on Earth (they may be up or out there, but down here they are an inseparable part of all of life and our Being). Each Sign of the Zodiac has a planetary Ruler.

We may begin with Saturn, Ruler of Aquarius followed by Jupiter, Ruler of Pisces followed by Mars, Ruler of Aries followed by Venus, Ruler of Taurus followed by Mercury Ruler of Gemini, followed by the Moon Ruler of Cancer, then by the Sun Ruler of Leo, followed by Mercury, Ruler of Virgo, followed by Venus, Ruler of Libra, followed by Mars, Ruler of Scorpio, followed by Jupiter, Ruler of Sagittarius, ending in Saturn, Ruler of Capricorn as it is also Ruler of Aquarius.

SATURN: The Lord of the Planets

It is interesting to observe from the text above that the planetary pattern arising from the circular/spiral year possess an order of specific planets directly to the Sun, and then a return journey from the Moon with the same planetary order but in reverse:

SATURN; JUPITER; MARS; VENUS; MERCURY; MOON; SUN ; MERCURY; VENUS; MARS; JUPITER; SATURN.

The order of the planets begins with Saturn and ends with Saturn.

The first six Zodiacal Signs and planetary order is Yang/Male and Solar by nature, thus:

AQUARIUS-SATURN to PISCES-JUPITER to ARIES-MARS to TAURUS-VENUS, GEMINI-MERCURY to LEO-SUN*

These represent the first half of the Chinese New Year Cycle, and therefore the Zodiacal Signs indicated and the specific order of the planets may be valued as starting as Yang/Male in nature and therefore has much to do with ideas and theories.

The second or latter six Zodiacal Signs and planetary order is Yin/Female and Lunar by nature, thus:

CANCER-MOON to VIRGO-MERCURY* to LIBRA-VENUS to SCORPIO-MARS, SAGITTARIUS-JUPITER to CAPRICORN-SATURN.

These represent the second half of The Chinese New Year Cycle, and therefore the Zodiacal Signs indicated and the specific order of the planets may be valued as Yin/Female in nature and therefore have much to do with the manifestation of physical things - realities!

It will be noticed that the first six Signs end with Leo/Sun omitting Cancer Moon, whilst the second six Signs begin with Cancer Moon which then skips straight to Virgo/ Mercury, omitting Leo/Sun - this arrangement maintains the symmetry.

The first six Signs deal with ideas and theories, and the latter six Signs deal with Material practicalities - these are archetypal descriptions and in ordinary life these attributes may be somewhat mixed.

This is deliberate as Leo/Sun is Yang/Male and represents maximum Yang/Male at the time of The Great Heat, and the Cancer/Female Sign represents the beginning of the Yin/Female Cycle latent within the Yang/Male as explained above and reaching Her most powerful period at the time of The Great Cold.

It may also be stated that: Cancer/Moon is traditionally Mother and Leo/Sun is traditionally Father. This is normal Astrological Lore. Even so, this over-skipping reveals the exquisite linkage of The Mother & The Father, not only within astrological lore, but as the backbone, the core, to all of creation as we know it.

THE FIVE PLANETS POSSESS A DAY RULERSHIP AND A NIGHT RULERSHIP

Importantly, it may be perceived by the reader that the 5 planets (traditional planets) have a Yang/Male or Day Rulership and also a Yin/Female or Night Rulership.

Therefore, the planets other than Sun & Moon possess a masculine and a feminine principle whose manifestations for instance, taking, say Planet Venus; its Feminine side, bringing an interest in valuable possessions and beautiful things (which is Taurean), and its Masculine side bringing an interest in music, poetry and writing (which is Libran) - the Female side being concerned with the more material aspects of life, whilst the Male side being more concerned with interesting ideas and manifestations of perhaps an ethereal and of an abstract nature.

We may also conclude, and from the ancient Chinese point of view with esoteric knowledge from the Middle East, humanity is subject to:

A Daily Cycle of Male Yang and Female Yin. The Yang Male Cycle begins at Midnight local time, reaches its climax Midday, at which point, the Female Yin Cycle begins, reaching its climax at Midnight. Of course this fundamental law works interiorly within all living things. Indeed, such a phenomenon describes the common daily happenings - common to us all each day, but also analogous to the yearly cycle as stated above.

Actually, the moods of the day change every two hours, though because of the velocity of change involved and of daily life, these subtle changes may not be perceived totally by us humans, but are so perceived, by insects and other animal species, including perhaps by the nature of the different species of vegetation.

Of course there are many other types of Curious Cycles we are subject to, both by the nature of the exposition of the ideas above, but also by other World Systems that exist within corpuses of knowledge belonging to other Traditions.

The Cogent argument of this exposition is to convey to the reader the notion that with All & Everything, Male/Female; Yang/Yin; Heaven & Earth; Sun & Moon; Father & Mother are inseparable and should enjoy therefore equal regard - one is neither inferior nor superior to the other.

Nothing can exist without these exquisite but fundamental arrangements - even the Signs of the Zodiac which determine the nature of all phenomena for us on Earth and beyond, alternate with first a Masculine Sign followed by a Feminine Sign followed by a Masculine Sign and so on.

ENLIGHTENING SATURNALIA - PART TWO

(Some repetition with added material)

I have been asked to explain further the Roman Saturnalia's pre-Christian Eras relevant dates, and other important matters in content:

With our present Gregorian (Pope Gregory VIII 1582) Calendar, the 60 days of darkness, contemplation and reduced activity, begins more or less around 21st December (Winter Solstice - shortest day) and continues for 60 days until 18th/19th February of the following year.

There is a certain mathematical splendour given to us with regard to Creation, and a part of that glory, that breath-taking construct, is presented to us as the Heavenly Zodiac with its Twelve Divisions or Signs .

The Zodiacal Signs that are actually the spacial backgrounds surrounding the Earth from East to West heaven-wise are the 12 great '**divisions of life**' and each division covers a major **aspect** (see below) to the manifestations of existence.

Thus, twelve major life **aspects** present all possible features, items, issues, subjects and objects in creation, and in the world, and are all categorised within the Twelve Signs.

Sixty Days covers exactly 2 Signs of the Zodiac as each Sign of the Zodiac is traditionally and symbolically calibrated with 30 equal days in length. This totals up to the 60 days.

The relevant Zodiacal Signs associated with the 60 days total, are Capricorn for the first 30 days, and Aquarius for the second 30 days. Both these Signs of the Zodiac side by side are ruled by Planet Saturn. As with all Planets (Planet from the Greek meaning: Wanderer), Saturn has a Male and a Female manifestation. The Female manifestation - night, is given to Sign Capricorn, and the Male manifestation - day, is given to Sign Aquarius.

TWO **ASPECTS** (of Saturn); **ASPECTS** AS REFERRED TO ABOVE ARE AS FOLLOWS:

How Cosmic Capricorn works for us, is through its inherent principles imposed on our lives as: caution and restraint and the recognition that success in all its forms comes with hard-work and the learning of lessons by the inevitable mistakes we make during our lifetime. Also, the appreciating and the Seeing of the long-view and the gaining of wisdom because of it. This means respect for the law in all its forms that assist the development of safety, fairness and justice for all. It means also the preservation of all that is good, and thus and therefore it rules Tradition - Tradition that brings stability to this unstable world. These attributes are the Feminine side of Saturn's influence where care, safety, security, civics and viability are dominant. The traditional but esoteric Element is Earth. Earth's true meaning psychologically: all that is mundane, practical and viable. Key word: Conservation.

How Cosmic Aquarius works for us, is through its inherent principles imposed on our lives as: the value of solidarity with the many, and the necessity of developing knowledge and skill whereby man and woman may enjoy the matters in life that have gravity, meaning, purpose, sanity, knowledge, and civility.

Through the Zodiacal Sign of Aquarius we enjoy the inventing of institutions that favour development in art, science, engineering, design, medicine and much more.

Also the dissemination of any of the intellectual gains from these subjects for the many.

It means the welcoming of the new if it is of true value to the world - Invention, Creativity and Altruism means that humanity does not stagnate or remain fixed and unmoving in its path and in its destiny.

Ideally, spiritual development should be simultaneous with technical development?!?!?!?! Whatever, these attributes are the Masculine side of Saturn's influence whence intellectual curiosity, learning, and dissemination of knowledge to uplift the mind of mankind, are dominant. The traditional but esoteric Element is Air - Air's true meaning psychologically: blue sky thinking/revelation. Key words: Inspiration/aspiration.

It may now be perceived by the reader that planet Saturn rules gravitas, seriousness and a sense of purpose to all things. Thus, the 60 days mentioned above has to do with deep thought, contemplation and meditation as suggested in my previous statement:

A Reckoning. Confidentially, monasticism and prayer is a Saturn invention - as mentioned above Saturn is the ruler of both Capricorn and Aquarius.

However, because these 60 days of seriousness could be such a drag to so many individuals, and particularly those tribal cultures that enjoy fun and excess - especially irresponsible fun and excess, such as with the behaviour of many of the ancient Romans, Saturnalia was established to enjoy 60 days of partying and debauchery to enable the getting-through of that most difficult time of year. A time of dullness in light and torpor in activity.

This worst and most difficult time of year, considered as such by many individuals, states and nations of that time, and perhaps of the present age, was to muddle through without suffering too much depression, by instituting fun and games, sex, drugs and rock n' roll over this 60 day trial of **guilt**. (See latter part of this book: Seven Deadly Sins).

Even so, in <u>modern times</u> for many of us, it calculates from 60 up to 365 days of profligacy, lunacy, dissoluteness, licentiousness, recklessness, Godlessness and prozac as normal. Ha ha!

In Medicine, words such as: Crepitus (a Saturnian word) from which we derive the word: decrepit, describes perfectly the deterioration of a bony joint that makes a grating sound when in re-articulation/action. Crepitus is the name given to that disturbing sound of wear and tear - a Saturn phenomenon!

Saturn being the Lord of the Planets is also described by the Ancients, quite rightly, as Father Time. The natural acceleration and deterioration in the process of ageing that none of us may escape, is ruled by Planet Saturn.

This is why the Ancient Greeks considered that the greatest gift to a person was his or her premature death just before reaching old age. Thus, could be avoided the indignity and the decrepitude and the helplessness of this last remaining epoch of a human lifetime.

It is interesting that musically speaking in Holst's - The Planet Suite, very rarely is the superb and sublime music that describes Planet Saturn is ever played. People do not realise what they are missing with this beautiful piece of music written by his genius Gustav Holst.

Throughout the piece the beat of time is emphasised most wonderfully and subtly with a profound sense of resignation as to the end of life that is revealed towards and at the end of the piece.

Of course, you may try as did the 120 year old man would do each night to avoid and to escape the Angel of Death's sweeping scythe. Because he ate two pounds of raw garlic every day, he was able to skip the calling.

When the Angel of Death entered the old man's bedroom at midnight and tapped his shoulder as he lay in his bed, the old man would turn his head around to breath at the Angel of Death profusely; saying to it as he pushed his breath out: "and who are you hoo hoo………"!

Further, what is generally not recognised by the medical profession both Orthodox and Alternative, is that CREPITUS need not be a normal feature of bony joint deterioration with most of us, regardless of what doctor says!

He/she is blissfully unaware that if our pelvises could be re-stabilised - most of them, [pelvises] being dislocated and that includes the reader reading this, then we would not suffer pain, arthritis and degenerating bony joints - all that can be happily avoided easily. For further understanding of this conundrum see: www.alexaligntherapies.com

WHOLESOME IS OUR PRECIOUS GENDER DIVIDE

Why have I written this Book: It is to clarify in mind, and to satisfy a heartfelt need, to reconcile several **contradictory** and **divisive** views between the world of the spiritual and the lofty, and the world of the temporal and the humdrum. As an example, this means:

The apparent contradictions within and from: politics to philosophy; science to religion; art to anarchy etc., etc.

This divisiveness, or in other words: the **apparent two points of view within a given subject seemingly opposed**, is never truly explained or even understood properly, and is cleverly side-stepped consciously or unconsciously by the authors and the commentators on all subjects that have inherent opposing views, whether written or spoken.

Without questioning or discussing the abstruse areas of these corpuses of knowledge, or the important contradictions within these given bodies of knowledge in subjects and, in objects, we perceive only separation and almost inevitable angst. This is because, there seem always to be two sides to an argument or a theory, and possibly a third argument though this may be either a product of the two opposing views when intertwined, or simple variations or shades of contradictions of the existing two points of view.

What has to be realised is that every **subject** may be either **Masculine** or **Feminine** in nature and in expression, and every **object** may be either **Masculine** or **Feminine** in nature and in expression, both Spiritual and Temporal.

Everything in existence has this exquisite division and therefore these two aspects of allotment are complementary because Male and Female in existence and within all phenomena, cannot function without the presence and the workings of each with the other. In other words, everything in existence which is either Masculine or is Feminine is one-half of a **Union**.

However, within everything in existence, humanity normally only sees, hears and perceives separateness and un-relatedness and any correspondence suspected between these two aspects of Male and Female is still perceived as separate and therefore contrary. What is rarely perceived by us in this miraculous division is its **complementariness. That is: As two sides to the same coin.**

My hypothesis is the **Law of the Complementary,** which has been forgotten not only in recent times but this forgotten law has been in oblivion since even before the Renaissance from the 14th century onwards? – certainly in the occidental world. It seems: that which is Masculine tends to be theoretical and that which is Feminine tends to be the more temporal or practical i.e.: Revelation (Masc.) v. Tradition (Fem.); Theory (Masc.) v. Practice (Fem.); Truth (Masc.) v. Proof (Fem.); Ethereality (Masc.) v. Mundaneness (Fem.), etc.,

This fundamental law for English Speaking Peoples has been most definitely forgotten, as already mentioned above, probably because of the neutering of the English language at the epoch of the Saxon Kings post circa 800 A.D.

Between 800 A.D. and 1150 A.D. under the Saxon Kings, nouns and adjectives in words lost their gender values, and thus, we have become over time insensitive to the Masculine and the Feminine division in all and everything in existence.

It happens that in all historical events and up to the present time, one gender, say, Masculine predominates politically and later as change takes its inevitable course a Feminine gender period predominates. Even so, a single gender dominance may be necessary at a particular historical time-period, though one might be right in thinking that a balanced epoch of nil extremes is possible under an equal gender regime.

Several things are certain in life for us all, and they are: Death, Taxes and **Change.** This means, that there will always be a change of the external matters predominating, as with the political system that underscores our lives which affects us all, or with individual life changes, that affect mostly that individual. This wave-change is normal and probably healthy, and is either Masculine or is Feminine in nature. That is, a mental attitude replaced with Mindfulness/Betterment and even with ethics, and/or a fundamental but re-development of actual structure both body physical and Politically System-wise (Reformation).

As a practical example of a balanced mix of Masculine and Feminine as modus operandi, we have at our present epoch two contra-points of view politically in the United Kingdom and neither viewpoint is able to dominate 2019. Because of this unusual circumstance, as outlined above, an agreement to meet in the middle, i.e. a compromise has been established by the two parties involved, and thus we have as a consequence a third element, or third point of view coming into being which probably pleases nobody with the addition of the malcontentedness of the demos (people).

Apart from the shenanigans of Brexit, there is the example of the coalition government in the United Kingdom and the execution of its policies (2010/13 A.D.); policies both Masculine and Feminine in their intrinsic nature, but did not please the many, especially the parasitic students who protested.

Masculine points of view are usually theoretical and abstract; and feminine points of view are usually practical and mundane and have to be exercised by us all, and these 'doing matters' are usually punitive.

Masculine points of view tend to be on the more freedom loving side and those of the Feminine tend to be on the more cautious and proven side of things. Towards right-wing politics tends to be the Masculine and with fewer restrictions, whilst towards left-wing politics tends to be Feminine and therefore subject to scrutiny and all the subsequent laws that will be passed to gain control. Just as a Mother's job is to discipline the children. This is because, amongst many things, She is the Queen of The Home, and that area is always best served by the Female.

Interestingly, when in Male or in Female extremes the very opposite effects occur - which is actually the intrinsic theory of Yin & Yang.

For instance, it may be argued that the rise of the extreme right-wing Nazi Party in Germany in the Nineteen Thirties was a direct reaction to the powerful and dangerous influence of Communism. Communism threatening the whole of Europe at that time epoch.

To take definitions of gender division further; its philosophy per se, and which is given a Masculine attribute, tends towards the theoretical and also examines ideas, and their place and purpose in creation.

Politics has to deal with the realities of the epoch in which individuals find themselves, and the Feminine attribute therefore has to attend to all the immediate practical and mundane intricacies and complications demanded by the society of that time and therefore by the government of that time.

Science as such, is a Feminine phenomenon, in that inherently it looks to the finding of the proof of an item's worth and its complexities, and also, the examination and calibration of a phenomenon and more.

Religion and metaphysics are a Masculine phenomenon, and as such, rely on the profound conviction of the need for humanity ultimately to encompass a wider view of life, its sanctity and its uniqueness, never to be taken for granted - it is an enlightened way of seeing all of life as Whole without too much emphasis on its many restrictions.

Blue sky thinking and more, is the inherent capacity to operate daily with conscience thereby allaying the needs to have more laws passed by government to restrain our freedoms. Libertarianism is rampant and is a direct result of the worst of human behaviour being out of control. Thus, government is required more and more to pass laws coded to restrain and constrain us.

The paragraph above reveals the very real dilemma of an <u>extreme</u> (libertarianism of *Yang*) becoming its opposite (strictures as dictated by *Yin*).

A REALITY CHECK FOR THE YOUNG
BUT ALSO FOR THE ADULT

On the subject of global networking, you will experience interesting phenomena when utilising Social Media and any other kind of internet communication because its usage may unwittingly embroil you into criminal activity by the hobnobbing and the cavorting, though innocently, with the low-lives of this world who use the internet for their own illegal and/or selfish gain - assuming you are not one of those very felons!

The criminals and the recidivists are abundant in number within the present-day's liberal ethos and are more cunning than ever in their dastardly behaviour. Remember, apart from the good, the Internet holds within it many strange and potentially wasteful activities as well as dangerous twists and turns cleverly applied by unbelievably astute and cunning minds - minds, especially those owned by the many miscreants that surround us.

It is a shocking indictment on mankind whose many members have turned a phenomenon of such wonder and such splendour as the Internet, and turned large swathes of it into the playground of vileness and criminality - criminality so abundant that our governments dare not tell us the truth about the cost in financial loss, in various ways to individuals to companies to economies.

It is true that the Social Media may allow you the possibility of making constructive business relationships and indeed a few good personal relationships.

However, there will be those internet users who will in reality waste your precious time, in other words, they will be feckless and indolent time-wasters.

Also those who have an ulterior motive, and who will solicit your friendship or your acquaintanceship, should hopefully, galvanise the need within you to be wary; because so many of these 'chancers' will not have the genuine interest in developing anything truly constructive with you, but only to generate mischief that will prove immediately or latterly a detriment to your life, mild or of deadly seriousness!

The reasons: 1. Dealings, and building relationships with these individuals may not be feasible as you are living in different countries or in vastly distant areas. 2. Fraud is rampant and abundant and because you are young and have not yet become experienced in suffering life's ability to pull the wool over your eyes (even the most savvy of us will be duped), you may become involved with financial transactions from which you may not easily be able to extricate yourself, if at all, when they are shown to be false, or they go horribly and dangerously wrong. 3. The reality of other peoples' professions/interests, may have no connection at all with the matters you actually have in mind.

In this way be careful of distractions and the wasting of precious time - wasting time; so commonplace with being online:

Waste Time

On-line

Obsess ?

Brain-less!

With his genius, Albert Einstein understood the nature of Time…He said:

"The reason for Time is so that everything does not happen at once"

Before you look round, time has vanished, and it is too late to retrieve this minute by minute fascinating phenomenon that to the enlightened amongst us is considered an illusion anyway.

Somehow Einstein knew that what we perceive and see normally as linear Time-Wise is actually, from another viewpoint, lateral…that is: The whole of existence, past, present and future exist all at the same moment!

Time as an entity is really only appreciated as we begin to Age: We are not taught at school that as we pass through our **Seven Ages**, the sense of Time actually accelerates in velocity as opposed to the dragging of Time we experience when we are young.

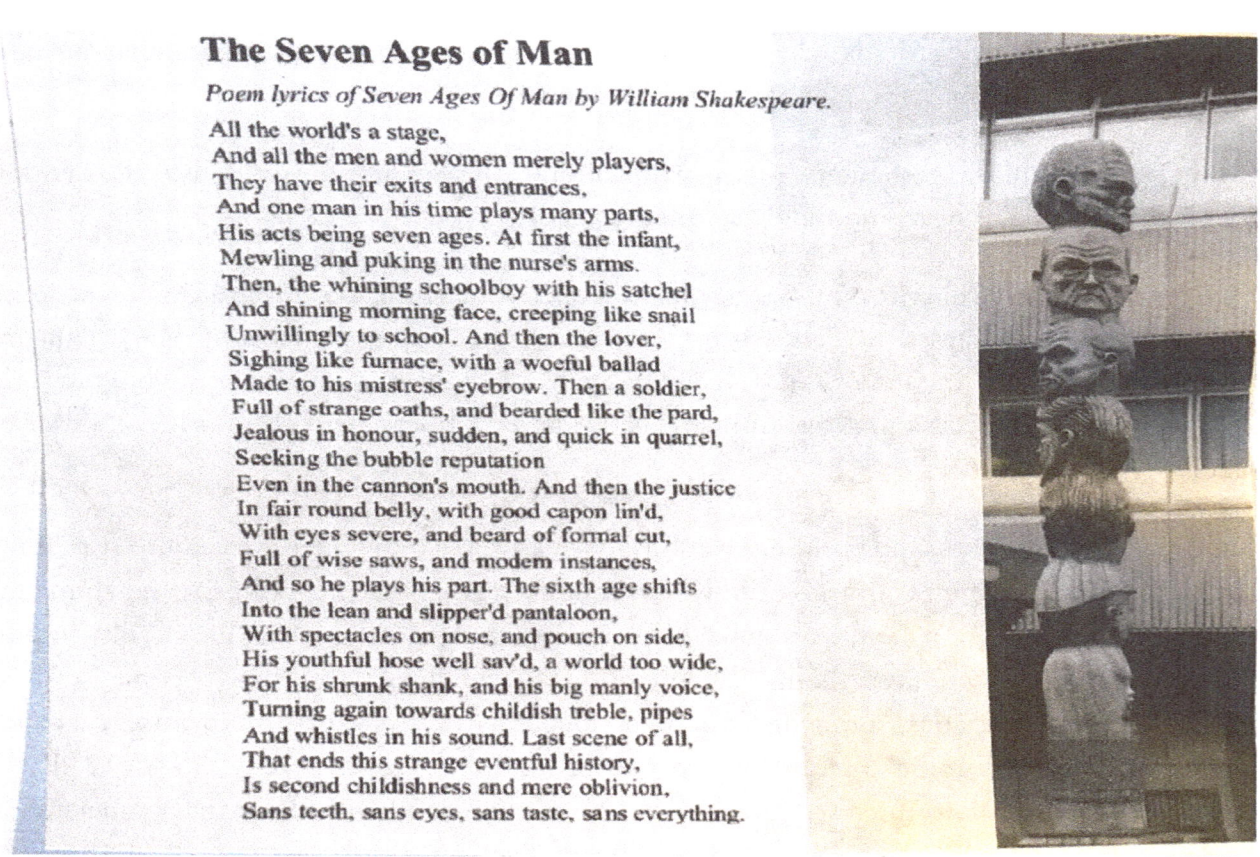

The Seven Ages of Man

Poem lyrics of Seven Ages Of Man by William Shakespeare.

All the world's a stage,
And all the men and women merely players,
They have their exits and entrances,
And one man in his time plays many parts,
His acts being seven ages. At first the infant,
Mewling and puking in the nurse's arms.
Then, the whining schoolboy with his satchel
And shining morning face, creeping like snail
Unwillingly to school. And then the lover,
Sighing like furnace, with a woeful ballad
Made to his mistress' eyebrow. Then a soldier,
Full of strange oaths, and bearded like the pard,
Jealous in honour, sudden, and quick in quarrel,
Seeking the bubble reputation
Even in the cannon's mouth. And then the justice
In fair round belly, with good capon lin'd,
With eyes severe, and beard of formal cut,
Full of wise saws, and modern instances,
And so he plays his part. The sixth age shifts
Into the lean and slipper'd pantaloon,
With spectacles on nose, and pouch on side,
His youthful hose well sav'd, a world too wide,
For his shrunk shank, and his big manly voice,
Turning again towards childish treble, pipes
And whistles in his sound. Last scene of all,
That ends this strange eventful history,
Is second childishness and mere oblivion,
Sans teeth, sans eyes, sans taste, sans everything.

THE SEVEN AGES (epochs of time) OF MAN offered to us above by Shakespeare in his very meaningful poem are:

(The Seven Ages Of Man Sculpture - Queen Victoria St., London by Richard Kindersley).

First phase of life: The Moon ruling the beginning and the early years of man. Second phase of life ruled by Planet Mercury. Third phase by Planet Venus. Forth phase by Planet Mars. Fifth phase by the Sun. Sixth phase by Planet Jupiter and the Seventh phase by Planet Saturn - Saturn as old age. These are Planetary Time Periods to which man is subject:

Further definition in understanding how the planets enter into this equation:

The Moon is ruler of our beginnings in that our traits and our characteristics are formed by the close family ties and influences which are immensely powerful in the first seven years of our life.

Planet Mercury has to do with our ability to learn and to communicate - the time we receive our basic education but leading to higher education as we progress.

As we begin to mature in late 'teens and into our 'twenties, the planet Venus takes hold. It does so by given us self awareness and bestowing within us important likes and dislikes that bifurcate into very particular or even peculiar tastes for the opposite sex and for the need to express ourselves creatively whether through personal interest (hobby) or work-skills.

Planet Mars dominates within the early mature years, in that we now know our talents and our potentials and we work hard to make our way in the world, usually because we are bringing-up a young family. It is a time of the great energy surge that urges us to be competitive and to achieve.

The reality of the radiant Sun-Star in an interesting way represents within us maturity and sturdiness. A maturity that has within it the knowledge that we the individual now know our direction in life, possessing the honesty and the integrity and the awareness of our limitations, but also our talents and our attributes.

In this way we pursue those things that have emerged deep from within and manifest them without, and this confirms the **true nature** of our Being.

Planet Jupiter represents that period when we may experience and enjoy our successes for all the work and the hardships that have brought us to this very expansive period in our lives. Everything gained in this epoch however, may be lost if bad judgement, bad luck, and unfortunate circumstances pre-manifested.

Planet Saturn represents, and is, the closing period of our lives, in that all the good and all the bad things we have done or not done, come to the fore and thus our wealth, our wisdom, our regrets and the things we leave behind for good or ill become uppermost in our minds, hearts and our bodies.

Returning to Social Media:

Regarding the making of potentially useful contacts via say: LinkedIn and with any other Social Media Agencies that may help your career to flourish, ultimately, it will be your face to face meetings that will prove most useful in business and otherwise. It is the personal touch and the personal relationships that succeed.

Go to meet your potential business associates, partners and contacts.....remember that first impressions count; you will never get a second chance. This is why you need to be pleasantly mannered, and importantly, dressed well and sensibly, but also it is good and right to be humble and attentive.

Ideally you should learn some basic etiquette. Pay absolute attention to the other party…do not but-in when having conversations.

You will find with the other party that the more religious those individuals are, they do happen to be a little more genuine, friendly and tolerant.

For instance, those people steeped in Catholicism and any other of the great religions, are generally well mannered, sincere and possess a quietness about them.

We have become almost devoid of these attributes in the present almost Godless society in which we live. Read: The Seven Deadly Sins end pages.

If you cannot dress tastefully, then seek advice from someone who knows how you should look. Even if you decide to become a Decorator, a professional skill always in demand, then dress in white overalls. Look the part.

You will be surprised how many people stop to ask your particulars about costs for decorating their houses and more, simply by looking the part.

Never dress casually in a formal setting. Never appear slovenly in connection with these subjects under discussion. Never be, and never behave as a hobbledehoy (nowadays they are everywhere to be seen). To be such, the harsh reality is that being out of place in this manner and behaving as do the chimpanzees, will destroy your chances of bettering yourself.

In your workplace, give yourself completely. Do not watch the clock. By giving yourself, selflessly, you will be noticed and earmarked for special duties and later promotion.

Work diligently, try not to get involved with the office politics.

Always ask your boss if you may be of assistance to him/her. Even if this means making them tea/coffee. Be humble and learn, learn, learn.

The bully is everywhere male or female. Never, never feel hard done by because you might be bullied. Take their flack as a gift - a priceless gift to enable you to climb the spiritual ladder which will increase your manhood or womanhood, as well as your knowledge and your wisdom and your capacity for tolerance.

It is only under pressure, and the bullying and the bad attitude of others that actually becomes a blessing to you - you may not see this at the time. You may feel 'hard-done by' - great mistake!

Under those interesting circumstances you will see yourself as you really are and you will see the need to make improvements to your character and to your body language and more.

Seeing yourself like this as you really are gives you two options: 1. You remain like everyone else, complaining, moaning and blaming everyone and everything else except yourself. or: 2. You take that attack in whatever 'which way' as a learning process, using it as a stepping-stone for better higher things.....you will then know what is meant by self-realisation.

Taking all of this a stage further: Within the outside world whose processes and activities seem to be falling apart, in that, whatever direction you look to, your thoughts and your feelings inevitably become depressed as you become aware of the sad state of the world. This reaction has to be destructive to your well-being and therefore your health; especially because you do not hear much about the good and the constructive things that are manifesting in the world also.

Even so, it should be better understood that in truth, the state of the outside world is a direct reflection, a manifestation of the negative thinking and the distorted feelings of us, the people, regardless of class, colour or creed - those Human-beings who rule us mirror our [the people] inner state of Being.

Our disturbed and restive inner state of Being that in this modern world is, no doubt, partly a result of our tendency to Godlessness, whence nothing is sacred anymore.

As arrogant humans, we, especially so within the Western World; because we interfere and try to change things and matters existentially, and because we think that ideally a thing and a matter should be done in a particular way, (because we have been conditioned with the Western Ethos), it is so easy to forget that we, as humans, need to change for the better our interior selves first and foremost - it is that interior change for the better in all of us that will change the outside world for its betterment. All of J. Krishnamurti's books and teachings emphasis this **Truth**.

I want to mention at this point something that few of you will be aware of, and that has to do with the English language with which you speak. Even though I have mentioned this several times.

Leading up to (circa) 900AD, nouns and adjectives possessed a masculine and a feminine significance in 'Old English' - names of items were either in Masculine or in Feminine form according to the character of those things. So too, were adjectives divided between the Masculine and the Feminine in gender.

Under the Saxon Kings, within this era mentioned above, over a 300 year plus period, gender in our language became somewhat neutralised. The exquisite difference or nuance between the Masculine and the Feminine slowly disappeared - most other languages of the world retain this beautiful and exquisite distinction.

The point I am attempting to put forward is that because of this 'neutralisation' to our language, we English Speaking People have become somewhat insensitive to the splendid difference of gender with our nouns and our adjectives and therefore obtuse to the wonderful separation of the Male and of the Female in life.

The menfolk in English Speaking countries tend to have a boorish even a crude attitude towards the Feminine aspects of creation - and with women in particular. This may indeed be due to the absence of, and the poverty in understanding the natural equality of the Masculine and of the Feminine as in the whole of creation: Everything in existence is either the Masculine or the Feminine (50% each). It cannot be any other way.

It should be of no surprise that the suffragette movement began within the United Kingdom. Such a powerful Organisation of solidarity reflects the bad Masculine attitude of neglect and lack of awareness of the need to recognise **equal respect** between the sexes.

However, because of the present-day beliefs well inside the 21st century, the balance of women dominating the departments of life of both the: Making It High In The Business World Of Both The Agony & Of The Ecstasy, and in The World Of Academia, and in the World Of High Powered Positions Within Institutions, of whatever nature, except for those women now in their 70's and 80's, this 'New Found Emancipation' For Women of the present day makes them blind to the price they are paying for this 'freedom' so called, and that sacrifice of which they are unaware is: Loss of grace, elegance, gentility, femininity and natural unsullied beauty - all a celestial gift to them that has immense power in life and especially so, over the Male species of us Homo sapiens. In the words of an important character in one of Wilber Smith's books:

"They [the women] are too strident and too masculine nowadays".... to be truly attractive to the opposite sex.

You will not hear about this dangerous topic in today's world, mostly because, man and woman actually cannot see this danger of both sexes become too alike - we are too much in-it! We are living it, therefore it seems normal.

We will be creating a country filled with spinsters, as men, or manly men, take Far-Eastern women as wives, lovers and girl friends, because, as yet, these beautiful women from the East both interiorly and exteriorly have not yet been contaminated with this ugly Western madness.

'.....and so my friends it would be wrong to think that because we have made great technological strides, we have made progress in our behaviour as human-beings - we do make terrible mistakes that have detrimental and fateful consequences especially affecting human attitudes and human well-being. As George Oshawa (founder of Macrobiotics) said: "What has a front, has a back". Meaning that an action must inevitably have a re-action.

Here is another quote from Albert Einstein:
"Imagination is more important than knowledge." (On Science).

THE SEVEN DEADLY SINS (IN LATIN LEFT) & THEIR LESSER GODS (RIGHT)

Superbia	(PRIDE)	Lucifer
Avaritia	(GREED)	Mammon
Luxuria	(LUST)	Asmodeusu
Invidia	(ENVY)	Leviathan
Gula	(GLUTTONY)	Beelzebub
Ira	(ANGER)	Amon, Satan
Acedia	(SLOTH)	Belphegor

PELVIS TO EARTH ALIGNMENT

The asterisks below refer to subjects that are explained at the end pages of this Essay. The explanations are written in Italics.

It is a great privilege that we Homo-sapiens have been endowed with an Osseous Foundation by the 'Powers That Be' in that the bony frame, the skeleton, has been given a **Base** (pelvis) - but it is a Base that is elevated according to the height of the individual. This Base or '**Foundation Of The Skeletal Frame**' is called: Pelvis. Pelvis (Latin) meaning: basin or bowl shape.

The pelvic structure is of immense importance for many reasons as it holds within it our organs of reproduction, intestines for final absorption of distilled food and drink, and what may be called: The Power-House - the vital energetic work of the kidneys*, assisted by the dynamic force of the liver organ*. In addition, the pelvis acts as the Regulator* to the osseous/bony frame the skeleton, in extraordinary ways and therefore to the body as a whole, but with the assistance of the Liver function.

The Foundation or Base, the pelvis, at its angular position, should always be **horizontal** especially when we as homo-sapiens are standing upright and erect, in relation to the other bones of the body, and is of Primary Importance - the horizontal collar bone or clavicle* that is parallel to it, is of Secondary Importance.

If we imagine an outward but plane trajectory extended from the horizontal pelvis, it parallels perfectly with the **Visible Horizon** of the spherical Mother Earth. (This is the dividing line engendered when the sky meets the earth).

This idea should reveal a wider and somewhat more, unseen, perhaps abstract or energetic relationship we all have with our Blue Planet. It is not an obvious connection but one that is there and just requires a little unfettered imagination to envisage.

Of the gifts of the Earth to us, it is not just the water we drink, the food that we eat, and the air that we breath, which sustains us, but the projected harmonious invisible geometric lines from our pelvises to the Earth's circumference we unknowingly are favoured with, that gives us extra support and nurture. This aspect of nourishment no doubt helps to strengthen us physically, emotionally and mentally.

This Earth's invisible way of nurturing, is also an additional stabilising factor for us, as **human animal beings,** to compensate us for being two legged creatures, as we are in truth, somewhat unstable physically, emotionally and mentally by having the ability to move around:

When we are compared to the plants of the vegetal world. All plants, like the trees, have roots that act as anchors for the plant's stability. Plants are planted, and cannot move other than by being swayed in the wind.

We homo-sapiens do not have the privilege of being fixed in one place. Being in one place always has an element of certainty and security about it - certainty in life that we humans just cannot get our heads around!

Gravity (That carries Heavenly Yang Chi*) is another stabilising factor given to us, as our bodies endure the pressure and the firmness of restrictive movement for our own good (saves us falling off the planet) except that when we suffer impairment of some kind, gravity is felt very much as inertia. This inertia or torpor, has a profound disabling effect upon us. Particularly so when we are **interiorly out of balance due to any of our vital organs suffering dysfunction of a particular kind.**

When our pelvises move out of kilter, or are moved out of kilter (contusion), this horizontality, as mentioned above, is compromised and thus, we are not consonant now with the earth's visible-horizon. This will have the depressing affect, as just mentioned, to our mental emotional and physical well-being and also, we are not really aware of the probable **cosmic implications?** This idea just proposed (Cosmos) will no doubt for some of us, be difficult to accept - proof, for a few of us is required, to allow general acceptance of this curious concept!

Gravity as we know it, is the medium, the carrier-wave employed to deliver Yang/Masculine/Heaven's force (read end pages). This Heaven's Force is cosmically centrifugal in character. Its action when applied to the mundane (when it hits physical matter) however, is always downwards and descending to enable its power to manifest and to innervate material things, and thus supply the **spark of life** to them, and in this way galvanise them into action/life*.

The invisible power of the Earth, is naturally Yin/Feminine and Cohesive*, and is centripetal in character. Its action, however, when applied to Heavenly matters is always upwards and ascending to enable its ramifications, usually in the form of structures both coarse and refined, to absorb the **spark of life** (Heaven's Force), and thus gain a foothold within these structures/ramifications enabling life as we know it to exist and to thrive*.

We have to bear in mind too, astronomically speaking, the fate of the world's inhabitants - that is, all living things - if there were no rotation of the Earth on its axis, they/we, would be crushed into oblivion.

The Earth whose natural forces are centripetal, but by its rotation around its own axis, converts these forces to move upwards and outwards in their ascent becoming centrifugal in action, counteracts the crushing downward and descending Heavenly force perpetually in operation by being carried by gravity. The Heavenly Yang Force is continually attracted to everything and anything that has physical properties.

Thus, Yin integrates with Yang and Yang integrates with Yin - this is the fascinating paradox of, and in life, and requires a clear mind and a concentrated study to comprehend all of its true inner and outer meanings.

In this way, Heaven/Yang attracts Earth/Yin and vice versa. This astonishing cosmic arrangement of compelling attraction, as is the positive pole of a given magnet to the negative pole of a different magnet, virtually cannot be pulled apart, then everything in creation has to be paired to be viable.

Outlined below are further discussions referring to the asterisks above.

Of the Kidneys, energetically they supply the fundamental motive force to all the other organs of the body assisting in maintaining their integrity and determining the strength of our **Constitution.** *When Kidney Chi is exhausted, usually in old-age, death ensues!*

Of the Liver, though anatomically placed on the right side of the hypochondrium, energetically its powerful influence determines the strength of all the functions within the abdomen below the umbilicus. Its work has to do with the proper employment or deployment of this precious energy or Chi that the kidneys create, hold and excrete. That is, a puissant liver will ensure good and sensible use of this treasured Kidney Chi which all the other structures and visceral organs require for their proper functioning.

Liver Chi has overall control of our strength and endurance. Needless to say, it assists total Regulation of the body's functions, but it is also involved most definitely with human emotions. The Liver Regulates all physiological functions within the body, viscerally especially. The Pelvis, though, Regulates the bony frame (skeleton) and therefore all physical movement.

As the Regulator to the whole body, the pelvis is likened to a weighted spinning wheel, but its actual motion is both up and down (superior/inferior) hip-wise - this motion is emphasised especially as we **walk***. Walking being of the utmost importance and a splendid form of exercise.*

Every machine has a built-in Regulator. Every car for instance has a flywheel, fixed usually at one end of its engine's crank-shaft - it is there to regulate the motion of the engine by storing kinetic energy to enable it [the engine] to run smoothly. Some of you will remember the old road steam-rollers with their enormous wheel shaped cowling above and at the side of the main engine. Within it is its flywheel for the smoothness of the steam-engine's motion.

Further, as mentioned above, within our mammalian bodies, one of the functions of the energetic (Chi) affects of the Liver is to take charge and to act as policemen to the whole body, ensuring continuity of the body's total functioning.

It is also not surprising that the energetic work of Liver Chi therefore, has great influence within the very lower portions of the body, particularly below the umbilicus, as mentioned above, to assist the Regulation of the movement of the pelvis, in this way enabling smooth motion of the lower and the upper parts of our bodies. This has to include the healthy functioning of the components of the abdomen generally - and also includes excellent performance of the sexual organs.

It is more than likely, that in the early days of developing humanity, the Elders of tribes and of clans and of subsequent nations that came into being understood the need to develop **native dancing** *precisely to keep good Regulation to the pelvis, and therefore to the body and especially its lower parts. All nations of the world have or had their native way of dancing; alas in modern times, these incredible dance spectaculars are forgotten or almost forgotten and especially so as regards to their* **prime purpose.**

Taking this Regulation aspect to a cosmic level, scientists know, and have known since the 1960's that Planet Jupiter has, as part of its cosmic function, the capacity in its extraordinary way, to bring back to normal the cyclic rhythm to other planets and moons within our Solar System, that have deviated from their normal rotation and/or circuit around the Sun. A deviation from the norm that may happen engendering an anomaly within the Solar System's construct - and these deviations do happen for many reasons, though mainly from the mixed gravitational pushes and pulls from inside and from outside of the Solar System itself. Planet Jupiter polices these irregularities and the norm is restored. Returning to Lock-Phase is the scientific term used.

> *Esoterically speaking, as each visceral organ in the body is ruled by a different planet, as are the days of the week, it so happens that Planet Jupiter is Lord over the Liver organ and its functions. This is on a physical and on a psychological level in mammals especially !*

Of the clavicle *that is parallel to the horizontality of the pelvis, it mimics the pelvic movement but in reverse, in that, if say, the pelvis rises on its right side walking-wise, the clavicle will descend by the same number of degrees on its right side. The same is true also when the pelvis rises on its left side, the clavicle will descend on its left side.*

If the pelvis is stuck on one particular side having ascended (superior), then the clavicle on that same side will tend to remain descended (inferior). Hence, the shoulders appear deviated from the norm; pain probably ensuing. Of course we are talking about the dysfunctional pelvis totally commonplace and leading to all types of back-pain and other musculoskeletal aches and pains - lovely! Leg length discrepancy is always a feature of bony pelvic dysfunction.

Heavenly Yang Chi is many things, but is best held in the mind as being the Masculine Creative Force that innervates, vitalises and galvanises all things and in this way generates life, within life's myriad forms.

Earth's Yin Chi is many things, but is best held in the mind as being the Feminine Force that supplies the structures and the ramifications of all things, and this enables the Heavenly Masculine Force to manifest and to give purpose to these structures and multifarious forms to enable mundane existence as we know it.

Look at your mobile telephone that is a Yin/Female structure, but quite dead without Yang/Male electricity to bring it alive. Without structure, Yang energy is without purpose and nothing is possible. Neither Yin nor Yang can exist without the other - a perfect marriage; a perfect union!

Further, on the Cosmic theme of the 'REGULATOR'

If we take the Moon and the Earth connection, then we should consider that the Moon acts as The Regulator to the Earth, as it forms a lattice web of sorts in its monthly path around our Mother Earth. This Regulation by the Moon to the Earth is essential because, without the Moon's input, the Earth's motion on its axis and on its elliptic journey around the Sun would be so unstable as to make life on Earth impossible to endure and therefore to obtain.

In addition, as the Moon rules the minute by minute timing with life's fecundity, our Blue Planet Earth would be sterile and without life.

*Further, in the same way, but on a much larger scale, The Planets as such, conduct essential Regulation to the Sun. Without the Planets operating as **servants** to the **Sun**, it [The Sun] would be unstable, such, as to disallow life to take place anywhere within its Solar System.*

THIS LAST CAMEO MAY BE CONSIDERED AS THE SUM TOTAL OF ALL THE PREVIOUS ESSAYS WITHIN THIS COMPOSITION

THE ESOTERIC LAWS GOVERNING THE FEMALE GENDER'S ATTRACTION TO HER MALE COUNTERPART!

It is understandable how the male is enchanted by the female, but for women to be captivated by the menfolk may be considered paradoxical. It is essential to keep in mind that I am working with the hidden but etheric tenor that determines our fundamental attraction to the opposite sex; and the following writings may offer a glimpse into the extraordinary laws governing the oxymoron of the female and male relationship.

Women seem to be attracted to the Male Form and Maleness. Yet his body formation is coarser and rougher than hers; hers is more refined and almost hairless, indeed, less of the animal in her. It is understandable that he is attracted to the more delicate and the more graceful physically rounded partner to counteract the rigour he suffers within the outside world - worldliness that has its frenetic, exhausting and frightening aspects.

Yet in truth he wants mostly from his counterpart warmth and comfort; the very things that he cannot obtain within the throng of the external world, even though he is built physically and mentally for the challenges to it - this being the outer world of life reflecting the agony, and the ecstasy as opposed to the close family realm of privacy and recline.

His arrival on Earth, having been issued from the refined and pure Heavenly dimensions, takes-on a mundane and a strident body and mind but with very great enthusiasm. Enthusiasm and alacrity, because the fundamental Law Of Life dictates that opposites will attract urgently, fervently and with passion. Take two magnets, each with its positive north and its negative south. The North Pole of one will stick like glue to the South Pole of the other with astonishing strength - such is a metaphor for every subject and in every object in our Universe:

A Phenomenon that is Masculine in nature may come into being or into reality, only when it is paired with another Phenomenon of the same species that is Feminine in nature.

The point being that:

He descends from Heaven's purity and with his ethereal body and pure state of mind and because of these qualities is immediately attracted to Earthly, even coarse matters (Heaven attracts Earth and vis versa as intimated in the RUBRIC below). He takes-on an animal-like body, and also a mind as yet unrefined - perhaps his refinement will take place if he is good enough to experience a redemption during his lifetime, and/or he is brought-up with high-cultivated persons about him. This will ensure his steady return to Heavenly pure things during this particular incarnation.

She is born of Earth, and since Earth attracts Heaven, she is compelled by her interior but urgent impulse to purify and to cleanse all the mundane matters about her. Thus, she naturally ascends, and is ascending indeed, from the beginning of this incarnation. Therefore she acquires a refined body and a clear, pristine mind. Her ascent to Heaven is so very compelling from her childhood onwards, that she, as with most women, does not require so urgently the Canon Laws of Life to control her. Whilst the menfolk, require these laws, at least to control their minds and their hearts which are normally influenced by their newly acquired **guile**. Guile that Earthly matters powerfully engender. (That is: Earthly matters into which he has descended). As it says in The Good Book (Talmud): 'Man is born with the evil impulse'!

The question arises from out of the texts above: How may a woman be attracted to her counterpart who, in reality, is primitive in body and, intelligence - initially anyway? (with a few exceptions!).

It is true that women throughout history have been magnetically attracted to men who ooze sacredness - these usually are 'men of the cloth' as they emit a gentle radiance that is engaging to certain kinds of women; the clergymen's openness does not seem to pose a threat to them - to the ladies that is.

Such behaviour with these particular species of men inclines some of them [men] to make overtures to any of the attractive womenfolk about them. The extraordinary story of the Russian Monk Rasputin and his interesting proclivities is a perfect example of this.

Vulnerable women and highly sexed religious men have through the ages been found In-flagrante delicto - observed even within the church interior and its shadowed corners.

Of course, it is not only the 'men of the cloth' who may engender a frisson within some womenfolk, but also with men who are strong and powerful because they possess the gift of charisma and/or mammon, or both - usually both!

Then there are those class of men who are deeply spiritual, but do not not actually practice any formal religion and it is their free-spirit in addition, that acts as a magnet towards certain women.

What does the average woman see in the average man? Perhaps it is his vulnerability - he has to put-on a show to be attractive to the female rather similar to those of the Birds of Paradise who prance about to attract their mate that is not too dissimilar to the observing of the behaviour of restless and restive lunatics! Thus, exaggerating certain qualities that he does (man), in reality, not possess!

Women perceive weakness effortlessly. Perhaps this is one of the features that attracts a woman to a man, even if he happens to be uncultivated, tramp-like and feckless.

She consciously or unconsciously has the notion that she has the power to make all things better for him both with his inner life, but also with his outer life. That is, his destiny career-wise and more.

Of course it helps if there happens to be what is called: chemistry between Him and Her. That is: Root and Branch Chemistry between them that is favourable in maintaining powerful mutual harmony. If fortunate, this disposition may be so puissant that it never declines, and it maintains their love throughout their lifetimes.

Even so, why does a woman find a man attractive in the same way that he finds her irresistible taking into consideration the discussions above?

Before further discussion, I direct the reader to the RUBRIC below that may supply the key to the greater comprehension to this very difficult subject; bearing in mind that the reader may need a glass of port and a cigar to get him/her through it!

RUBRIC:

The diversity of all Phenomena - Phenomena that are constructed in varying degrees of physicality, are the reflections, the counterparts of the conceptions which of course are ideas, but in abstraction, and which are also ethereal and therefore opaque and in this way are all formless as from the outset.

*Put another way: Materiality in its varying forms is the physical counterpart - the material evidence of the notions that come into being within the nebulous, rarefied and invisible dimensions traditionally called by many as: Heaven, as opposed to the Temporal world traditionally called by many as: Earth. (Heaven v. Earth).

* Note Algorithmically: Just before we undertake anything, the idea of it manifests first, and that notion directs the coming into being and the material evidence of that visualisation: Further, material evidence, but it was a abstract thought at its foundation.

Heaven is deemed as Masculine (Yang) and Earth is deemed as Feminine (Yin) - just as in the sphere of music: European Music Academies consider Major Mode as Masculine and Minor Mode as Feminine.

Immaterial Heavenly things begin to descend and as they descend, they take-on forms in varying degrees of temporal necessity and thus, Earthly matters begin to dominate and the original simplicity of Heavenly things becomes subject to excessive physical Laws and potential corruption as the descent reaches its completion.

Menfolk love these Laws as they offer employment for the use of their hands and for enabling them to exercise their brawn. Generally, anything mechanical and somewhat messy, is taken-up by them allowing the possibility of making life on Earth tolerable and liveable - a clever universal arrangement.

With womenfolk, they uplift their primitive surroundings to make them as Heavenly as is possible by bringing cleanliness, beauty and grace round and about. This is achievable, by encircling themselves with lovely things such as with flowers and sumptuous (if possible) settings - this having also, a civilising effect upon the menfolk.

Of course, I write of archetypes and we are not all archetypal. Some menfolk naturally seek refinement and to cultivate themselves, some womenfolk seek what is sometimes known as: Muck and Bullets especially nowadays!

To continue: The Chinese Symbol of Yin/Yang contains immense universal significance, and within that vast purview, <u>gender relationships also.</u>

White represents Masculine Chi and Heaven. Black represents Feminine Chi and Earth:

It is necessary at this juncture to define, as much as is possible, the word 'Chi': Chi is a vivacious translucent energy, but in many forms that drives and sustains life in all its possible combinations and which underlies and subsumes everything in existence - similar to the effects of Gravity that is everywhere both within and without with its effects. Even these statements above are limited viewpoints of the functions and purposes of Chi.

Heaven Yang Chi white (left side) constitutes the bulk of the upper figure but tapers-off as it descends within the circle but reveals also the weakening of its Yang Chi power as it descends and this declining potency may be calibrated in ratios. Fascinatingly, dead within the centre of the great Sea of Yang Chi (Heaven) atop the figure above (left) is a minute circle of Black.

This represents the small but powerful Yin Chi Feminine aspect of Heaven that by nature urges the Sea of Yang Chi (Heaven) to descend to enable it [Yang] to manifest itself in diverse ways in and on Earth, but also to innervate Yin Chi to enable temporal diversity as it (Yang) descends - how clever and perhaps devious, is the Yin Chi nature - deviousness, an attribute of the Feminine character and necessary in the scheme of things and is not meant as a reproof but as a compliment!

As Yang Chi descends its opposite number Yin Chi Earth black increases; meaning, amongst other things, that physical laws become more plentiful as Yang's descent is completed and at best this means Yang Chi becomes diversified giving life to all and everything that has a material basis (Yin Chi).

However, at worst, its inherent freedom being curtailed by more and more laws, (Yang Chi), may stifle spontaneity and even 'put the fire out' - for its Chi is seriously weakened as it is subject to more and more temporal laws - temporal laws: Yin Chi Earth.

Our democratic System of Government takes an idea (Heaven?) and gives it form (Earth), but as so many possible complications are brought to the fore that, the idea brought forth, eventually turns-out to be far from what it was supposed to be when it is, the idea, to be realised in actual physical and workable reality.

It is the defects of government when every interested party within it, must have its say on the matter at hand. (In the sense of The Elephant In The Room!).

We witness, if we are honest, in this democratic age of confusion and madness, the terrible flaws of our governmental system that breaks-down when extremely important issues arise that have a bearing on the direction of our Nation. Confidentially, when this happens, **certain kinds of Dictatorships directing the way forward may be forgiven - as with the needs and essentials of The War Cabinet/Council.**

In truth, our Governmental System is not, what it is cracked-up to be. We are told as from the Cradle how wonderful it is, and our politicians love to play on the cogency of this point.

The reality is something else or has become something else. We are witnessing a certain kind of Civil War but without the physical weapons to go with it?

The weapons employed now are vituperative and insultive. Engendered amongst the people are the worst of human emotions.

In quiet moments, we the people, will look back with shame at the display of ugliness in all its aspects, when eventually the present impasse with Brexit is finally resolved; or if not, I suggest we should look back with embarrassment and remorse.

This necessary repentance may to some extent assist our personal redemptions - personal redemption that should be a must in this day and age. Menfolk in particular may only move-on progressively when they have suffered a set-back that has had a profound effect on their lives, sufficient to send them into a different but better trajectory that is truly meaningful and that gives them a reason and a purpose to exist, because their conscience has been shaken and thus: woken-up!

Within a number of different religions, it is known that certain ethical texts may only be given to those men who have turned 40 years in age, because, usually by then, they have lived 'a bit' and have even gained a modicum of wisdom, as they should have experienced already up to that point in age the 'Slings and Arrows of the Outrages that Life throws down and into their/our paths' - into our paths with great gusto, and so they are meant to be.

Women do not have the same or do not need the same life-curve, they are under different laws - different laws that allows them a glimpse of truth that they tend to follow anyway. Thus, women are naturally somewhat more civilised.

Returning to the extraordinary Symbol of YIN/YANG above:

Now, Yin Chi Earth black is at its most powerful at the foundation (right-side) of the symbol. Deep within the Sea of Yin is a minute but intensely strong Yang Chi white circle.

It is the nature of this Yang Chi spot to urge irresistibly the Feminine Yin material elements to refine bit by bit by their ascent until total ethereality is reached back and up to the Sea of Yang Chi top left.

In this way, material things have been refined, justified and redeemed. Interestingly, the Feminine aspect may ascend and therefore suffer only one journey! The Masculine aspect must suffer two journeys - He has to descend first (left-side) to reflect Heaven but in temporal ways as he descends, and then to be redeemed totally on the journey of ascent (right-side) through the Feminine Yin material attributes. A perfect but beautiful if not elegant arrangement within our life construct - in my opinion!

This means that the Feminine Yin modus operandi is to carry the Masculine aspects of creation and to lift them into, and up into, the supreme high-order (Heaven). In this way, She is compelled to shoulder the Masculine alibi/motive until He is fully redeemed through refinement of all temporal matters, but up-high within the symbol's apex towards its top left side for the cycle to begin again only with greater urgency and to be expressed differently between each and every (yearly?) cycle - differently in the sense of a progressive evolutionary movement. For example: it may be God's will that as long as humanity survives another 500 years say to 2,520 A.D., it is likely that it [humanity] will be mostly light coffee coloured and slightly Far Eastern looking (eyes with slight epicanthic fold)! Meaning the almost total integration of most of the races of the Earth! This idea will be abhorrent to some, but it may be part of God's plan - who is to say?

Now, to the original question as to why a woman finds a near troglodyte man to be attractive sufficient to have an intimate relationship with him and also with him, meaningful sexual intercourse?

<u>It is because:</u>

It is well to understand how man may love and embrace a woman who is soft, vulnerable, feminine, warm, round and shapely which is an aspect of Yin Chi manifested, but why a woman may be attracted to the very opposite of these attributes - qualities that are angular, abrasive, direct, craggy yet straight-lined in overall shape which is an aspect of Yang Chi manifested, is because in truth (and the truth is

hard to bear) She desires to be directed, protected, innervated and dominated and these qualities may only be supplied by the more stronger, hardened, determined, resolute, independent, assured, and the more worldly Male partner of our species.

Thus, the bearing and the look of a <u>normal</u> male is paramount to gain the affections of a <u>normal</u> female. As She is round, malleable and yielding, He should be square, resolute and withstanding. These are the qualities she instinctively looks to - qualities which have to be the very antithesis of her interior feminine ethos.

Why then does this man go for this woman and not that one and vis versa? A man may have all the masculine attributes as above and a woman may have all the feminine attributes as above, but an attraction between them may not exist. Therefore something extra, some additional ingredient is required.....

'......and that is: the chemical reactions of one, being consonant with the chemical re-actions of the other. Chemistry is the material Yin aspect reflecting the resplendent spirit of the Yang aspect. The Spirit/soul whose residence is within the liver organ, is the prime determinant of sexual attraction. Put another way: the chemistry, so called, **is the material evidence of the dictates of the spirit.**

The primary re-action of a female person to a male person and vis versa is: 'Hmm, I like the look of her/him', but later the deeper layers of perception kick-in and it is these that determine whether the relationship should obtain at some length. Even so, the higher ethereal attributes of the Liver Function are the determinants whether it be a superficial attraction or a deep attraction; deep attraction that will have a time stamp attached to it - time in the sense of a lifetime partnership or a relationship lasting only for a number of months, or enduring for a number of years.

NOTE: It is one of the functions of the visceral liver to perceive, and in this way determine Male/female attraction. This organ with its gall-bladder has much control over the functions of the eyes and what they perceive - it is **vision** first that determines like and dislike as regards to the sexes. Other organs are involved, but liver and gall-bladder are the dominant determinants. Our real-selves; our souls (the ethereal and real part of us) never dies but resides within the liver organ and especially so at night when we are resting.

END

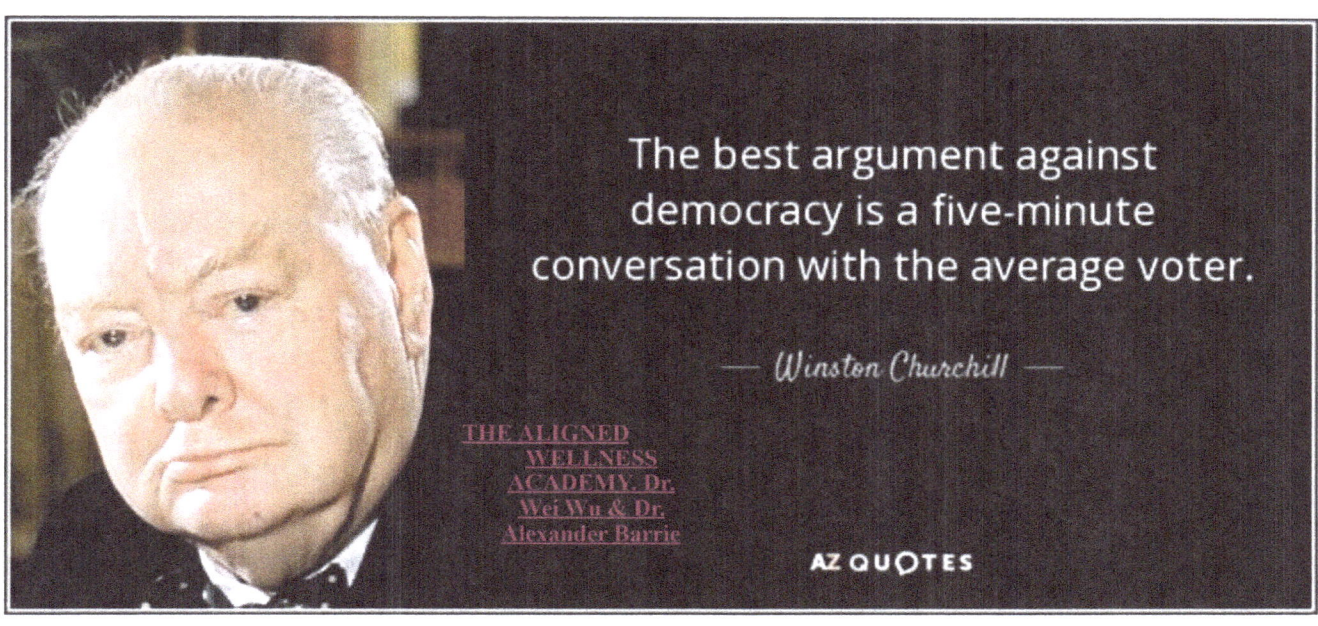

The best argument against democracy is a five-minute conversation with the average voter.

— Winston Churchill —

THE ALIGNED WELLNESS ACADEMY, Dr. Wei Wu & Dr. Alexander Barrie

AZ QUOTES

POSTSCRIPT

SUPPORTING OUR IMMUNE SYSTEM - PLUS DIVULGENCE
Dr. Alexander Barrie. 23/3/20 London.

*We are bombarded, information-wise, from all quarters as to how we may reduce the possibility of contracting this globally, thought to be accursed, **Coronavirus**, but also to learn the different ways we may bolster our Immune Systems to reduce the risk of contagion.*

Those of you, very few actually, who are acquainted with Prof. Rupert Sheldrake's: Morphic Resonance, will remember that within the contents of his book, reworded: A species of tree that has contracted a disease, in an especial way, appears to send a warning to all other trees of the same species, in all the different areas of the Globe* to enable that species to prepare and to defend itself, sometimes successfully, sometimes not. The Professor speaks of: The Collective Unconscious. Think of a deep memory, of which we are hardly aware, that is mainly hidden but ready to manifest into consciousness when primed to do so. It is the transmission from one tree to another with a message that is for us difficult to comprehend. Many of us find it hard to understand the means by which this message may be delivered. It is apparent that there has to be a electrical/magnetic field of sorts that presents the medium by which this message may be transferred - an aspect of Collective Unconscious: Physicists may call it: The Morphogenetic Field.

My point being, that this plague-like disease (COVID-19) travels, as a wave travels affecting all and sundry as it undulates across the globe - affecting some people more penetratively than others. In other words, as we are of the Homo sapiens species, we will all be affected slightly, mildly, or even fatefully, because as with the vegetal world (as revealed above), we the people, though of animal origin, will suffer similar consequences, being of the same species, no matter of what part of the world we inhabit.

How this 'other worldly' contamination travels to affect same species of organic material, is to some extent discussed above, but the whole matter is open to debate. Life is a mystery indeed, and the the more we learn and to understand it, the more questions arise, and many of the true answers to our questions are as elusive as ever - this is the beautiful and magnificent paradox of life! "God moves in a mysterious way. His wonders to perform" (William Cowper).

What I am saying is, that as Homo sapiens, we have already all been touched with and by this virus - this virus of torment. The sneezing, coughing and contaminated droplets from our fellow-men do not make the slightest difference as to whether we as individuals go down with this disease or not - it's already beside and inside us.

The disease's toxic manifestation depends on our propensities, our proclivities, which allow its full development within us or not as the case may be.

For some, it will mean death, for others, a few weeks of illness, and for the majority of us, just a disruptive nuisance, producing a few dry coughs, sore throats and a few sneezes here and there.

Thinking as to how this Coronavirus penetrates those individuals who have **not** travelled to other parts of the world where the virus is rampant and/or never been close to one who has contracted the virus, developed or still incubating, the reason, possibly may now be understood as outlined above.

This whole subject of transmission, so fascinating requires further development, because it reveals the connectedness to all things, and as to why the current ethos or way of thinking of man for good or ill, seems to be, or becomes: Universal - in other words, the way people are thinking and feeling around the world is actually, and in the round, the **SAME. This is with any subject under the sun, not just with viral contamination.**

Politically, the governments of the world, advised by their scientists, are making life much more difficult to endure by driving home the need to isolate ourselves and to lockdown. This in my humble opinion is the worst possible measure taken, and indeed, foisted onto and into the people - the people would and could do nothing but suffer.

Life should go on as usual, no disruptions, trade and communications as normal. Because, when this madness ceases, we, society will have little to return to - economies crashed, and bankruptcies - whatever assurances we get from governments in the end is all tat and meaningless, the meanwhile.

Those who fall ill, should retire to their homes and have bed-rest until they recover. The love and support of their families will see them through, but also, they must keep very warm, this includes the drinking of hot substances as with GINGER to create interior heat that will support the body's defences, but also to help extinguish the virus that is easily destroyed by heat sources. **See below things we should and should not do****!

Our way of thinking, our fears - fears increased by the news issuing from the media, government and their scientists, has to damage our immune systems, leaving us wide-open for this extraordinary virus to develop interiorly within our bodies (there is a plethora of scientific literature that confirms this awful connection of worry leading to illness). If this Coronavirus was/is so dangerous, as we are led to believe, since it is already beside and inside us, we should all be dead by now, with people dying and lying in the streets as they did at the time of the medieval historical Black Death!

There is another consideration, unpalatable to the many, and that is:

Probable mass-hysteria; the kind of derangement that gripped a large percentage of the British Nation at Princess Diana's death. This form of stupidity amongst the masses, has dramatic consequences as to the general health of the demos.

Confusion and mis-information seems to be present now affecting people en masse by many of them actually expecting to contract the virus in question, and with some people consciously or unconsciously actually looking forward to coming down with it (Death Wish).

This may explain why some younger citizens are infected with it - the younger generations do not have the stamina and the endurance of previous generations and a few probably think it 'cool' to be ill with it **and to be part of the ugly flavour of the moment**. It is a human problem, that the easier the life for us, the weaker we become with added sentimentality piled-on. Our affluent societies in modern times have conveniences and safeguards that never existed just a hundred years ago - and because of this, many of us are psychologically feeble as well.

*it seems that the countries most affected by Covid-19 are the ones in and around the North 40th Parallel. You may draw a vector around the globe at this latitude and you will be surprised how relevant it is, revealing those countries suffering most with this pandemic. Presumably, it would, for whatever reason, be the same in predominance at the South 40th Parallel with the countries of Southern Australia, New Zealand, Argentina and Sth. South Africa affected mostly. North and South of each of these fortieth parallels the virus in question has marginally less effect. There seem to be laws prevailing here that we just do not understand at present. It is also possible that the Earth's Jet Stream North & South and it's effects may be the means by which the transmission of both the bad and of the good influences, whether detrimental to universal health or favourable for universal benefit, are made!

****TO IMPROVE INTERIOR RIGOUR AND THEREFORE OUR IMMUNE SYSTEMS:**

The habits and items to <u>cease</u> doing or taking. Try to begin reducing at least:

1. Smoking 2. Alcohol consumption 3. Using Microwave Ovens. 4. Stop eating Refined Sugar & sugar generally 5. Stop Snacking. 6. Stop using Aluminium Utensils. 7. Stop Reading & Viewing material that is unhinging, subversive & deranging. 8. Cease Inner Negative Thoughts & Feelings that only damage our wellbeing and therefore our vitality and our Immune Systems. 9. Micro-waves from mobiles, tablets and WiFi systems - all lethal in reality; think about this. You should keep these necessities away from your body as much as is possible. It is probable that 5G**** already in operation in selected parts of the country will, in time, have a devastating effect on our body/mind - God help us! More about this below

Those habits and items to adopt or more enthusiastically so:

1. Eat only two meals a day. 2. Practice Intermittent fasting. 3. Chew your food and eat slowly with purpose. 4. In cold/cool weather, it is essential to keep warm. Be fully clothed always, and with undergarments. 5. Wear a hat and use a scarf to keep head and neck warm and safe. 6. Feet must always be dry - never wear shoes that let-in water. 7. Exercise always - the body was designed for daily motion. 8. Qi Quong means Effort & Discipline. Thus, this means any kind of movement and exercise. Exercising all joints is necessary and health-giving and effects favourably all visceral organs directly. 9. Preferably organic foods to consume where possible, but also fresh and fewer processed foods. 10. Outdoors in the light essential. 11. Adopt, read & study the Articles of Faith i.e. the sacred SCRIPTURES you were brought-up with and also, as with any of the Self-realisation Organisations.

My point being that answers to life questions are usually within the contents of religious SCRIPTURE. Apologies if I sound as though I am haranguing you - basically we humans require strict guidance because under the political regimes we live-in, in modern times, we suffer with too much guile - and worse, we cannot see this!

CONTINUING THE THEME OF THE THINGS WE SHOUD ADOPT:

Some of you know a bit about Pelvic Correction. Without our spines enjoying alignment, whatever we do to improve our Immune Systems, unless our spines and our pelvises are aligned, we just cannot reach that optimum state of health we should like to attain and which is our birthright to enjoy.

It is not only back-pain and all other musculoskeletal-skeletal aches and pains we suffer, but the more subtle aspects of our physiology not producing what we want and what we need that matters also. All those pesky Conditions/Ailments that beset our lives, many are due to misalignment of the pelvis and skeletal frame.

The pelvis is: The Foundation of the Skeletal Frame and it determines to a large extent the health of the whole of the human spine when integrated and aligned so that its horizontality parallels to the Visible Horizon. (this visible line is engendered when the sky meets the circumference of the earth) When this horizontality is projected outwards, on a plane to meet that horizon-line, there is balance and poise - This is one of the unseen connections to Mother Earth. Not to mention again that, the healthy spine assists us to suffer fewer illnesses as well as to give us flexibility of movement.

Certain items above require explanation. For example: Many of us professionals know that the use of Microwave Ovens for cooking your food is detrimental to health in that our blood's vitality is lowered, thereby leaving us open to the contracting of various diseases. Explanations on other items mentioned may be given if I am emailed and/or texted with questions, but we are organising right now online Courses to bolster our knowledge and also our Immune Systems generally. www.alexaligntherapies.com

Developing this mystery of *'virotic'* travel that does not seem to have a connection with a person infecting another person:

Just as an invisible message is sent from one tree to another tree of the same species, no matter in what part of the world they reside, in the same way, a *'virotic'* outbreak penetrating one, or a few people somewhere on the Globe will [perhaps] message latent viruses already lurking within hidden places and within people themselves but in entirely different areas of the planet [perhaps already residing deep inside our bodies] and ready to be aroused - rather like Sleeper Cells of the terrorists - and to do their dastardly work when called upon.......and in the terrorists case, encouraged to do their cowardly criminal corrosive activities because we ordinary human-beings are proven to be sentimentally weak and too much under the mesmeric laissez-faire of 75 years of peace and thus, lulled into a sense of unawareness of the lurking dangers of the Globe; this present-day weakness is taken advantage of by the felons of this world - we need to think as did Sir Winston Churchill, not to trust anyone or anything!!! The virus itself may be thought of as a felon indeed - **but is the virus the cause, or the result of ?!?!?!**

ARE PEOPLE FALLING ILL BECAUSE OF THE DEPRESSING NEWS THEY RECEIVE FROM THE PROFESSIONALS?***. THIS LOCKDOWN WITH THE MADNESS THAT GOES WITH IT, FOISTED UPON US BY OUR GOVERNMENT AND THOUGHT TO BE THE SOLUTION TO THE PROBLEM IS OF COURSE NOT YIELDING THE RESULTS AS WAS MEANT TO BE - NAMELY: THE DEMISE OF THIS VIRAL TRANSFERENCE. THE OPPOSITE EFFECT IS BEING PAINFULLY SUFFERED BY THE PEOPLE.

IT IS A COMMONPLACE OCCURRENCE THAT THE GOVERNMENT SOLUTION TO A NATIONAL PROBLEM - A PROBLEM THAT IS ODIOUS AND DESTRUCTIVE IN EFFECT AND WHICH MUST BE EXTERMINATED, ENGENDERS MORE PAINFUL AND DAMAGING ALMOST INSUPERABLE COMPLICATIONS THAT ARE WORSE THAN THE EFFECTS OF THE ORIGINAL PROBLEM - SO TOO WITH THIS 'VIROTIC' PLAGUE.

***Just observe the body language and the demeanour of the doctors and the nurses, their facial expressions - all sufficient to create panic and depression amongst the people. Life should go on as normal, without the sentimental attitude to death as we perceive it within the Occidental World. Death for most of us is a true and happy release, not a finite end, but another way we may redeem ourselves for the stupidities we have perpetrated in and of the present life. It is ironic, that the Indian communities living outside of their homeland India have adopted consciously or unconsciously all the ridiculous fears of and about, death, that we occidentals entertain and which are totally contrary to the natural ethos residing in India as seeing death as a happy release and a necessary part of life - Read: J. Krishnamurti.

***References: Dying To Be Me by Anita Moorjani. Many Lives, Many Masters by Dr. Brian Weiss.

Recommendations from *Psychologists*.

**1*. Isolate yourself from news about the virus. (Everything
we need to know, we already know).*

**2*. Don't look out for death toll. It's not a cricket match
to know the latest score. Avoid that.*

**3*. Don't look for additional information on the
Internet, it would weaken your mental state.*

**4*.Avoid sending fatalistic messages. Some people don't have the same mental strength
as you (Instead of helping, you could activate pathologies such as depression).*

**5*. If possible, listen to music at home at a pleasant volume. Look for
board games to entertain children, tell stories and future plans.*

**6*. Maintain discipline in the home by washing your hands,
putting up a sign or alarm for everyone in the house.*

**7*. Your positive mood will help protect your immune system, while negative
thoughts have been shown to depress your immune
system and make it weak against viruses.*

8. Most importantly, firmly believe that this shall also pass and we will be safe.... !

**'...........and now for the coup de grace as regards to the statements outlined above -
a shock to the conventional mindset: The Morphogenetic Field !**

The ancients were right! All phenomena good or ill may be deduced before it actually manifests simply by the calculations made from the planetary locations within our Solar System. This means the application of the values of the angular relationships the planets make to one another, every day, week, month and year as they follow their orbits around their master: **The Sun** (symbol⊙ circumpunct) all within our Solar System. This explains the significance of the quote: 'It's In The Lap Of The Gods'. ('......of Ancient Greek origin - the gods are the planets).

It is not realised universally as yet, that the positions of our planets at the time and the day of the New Moon that heralds the beginning of The Chinese New Year, marks the trend that will pan-out over that coming year as to its events and as to its character. The positions of the planets at this New Moon that initiates The Chinese New Year are of this utmost importance **secularly**, but not religiously, **for the whole world**.

Even the present day Chinese do not realise that their New Year is actually The New Year for the whole of the world as well, let alone the rest of the world not being aware of this phenomenon. You could say, that for whatever the reason, the Chinese have got it right as regards this extraordinary masterstroke. There are things/matters that the Chinese ancients understood, that are beyond our comprehension within our Occidental World thinking; just as their systems of medicine, so elegant, escape our understanding and our mindset.

In China itself, the early morning New Moon of Saturday 25th January 2020, signalled the beginning of The Chinese New Year. The planetary positions were unusual within a 24 hour window at this New Moon juncture. The planets involved and which seemed to be conjoined. In various angular positions, at this time period, according to ancient astrological lore, were: Mercury, Venus, Mars, Jupiter and to some extent Neptune all within a 2 degree arc.

The outstanding and most important configuration that day was between Venus and Mars, being at a 90 degree angle in relation to each other, but interestingly almost exact in seconds of arc. This is considered a very powerful connection indeed, but one that is fraught with dreadful consequences, in this case, for the world as a whole.

According to ancient lore, when planet Venus in its orbit reaches very close to the Earth, in its orbit [Earth], influenza may be generated as a pandemic amongst the earth's human inhabitants. In fact, checking the word Influenza in certain old style lexicons, the word Influenza is defined (paraphrased): 'as planet Venus comes close to planet Earth as in their orbits, they may cause a potential outbreak of the plague' - in this case: Influenza. Interestingly, Covid-19 is a nasty variation of common Influenza (if there is a common type!), but is still a respiratory infection and therefore may be fateful.

> **A little deviation here and a personal gripe:** With slapdash use of English nowadays we use the word FLU which is short for Influenza. To many of us, seeing the word FLU without an apostrophe ('flu) **judders the udders** so to speak. Even the respectable clinics and their doctors use the word FLU. Don't they they know it is bad English? Is it a case of the usual rubbish about maintaining the masses to remain in their blissful ignorance?

Returning to the fascinating subject about this very difficult configuration between Mars & Venus. We have known since the beginning of time that a 90 degree angle made between two planets generates rigour and dissonance - as to how these dis-attributes unfold accords to the nature of the planets involved and the Zodiacal Signs they are residing in at the time.

Positive Venusian traits produce harmony and friendship; appreciation of the Arts. Completion in relationships; abounding peace and wellbeing from which issues: stability in health. Negative Venusian traits produces vanity and self indulgence; sexual gratification without appreciation. Taking things for granted. Ugliness in behaviour that is an absence of awareness in offending others. Tardiness. Absence of self-caring and subsequently becoming a burden to others, especially in matters of health and wellbeing.

Irritated by the Planet Mars because of its caustic cosmic relationship to Planet Venus at the time of the New Moon priming the Chinese New Year to commence, has engendered and engenders within humanity internally and externally a prolonged period of discordance in many departments of life leading to unsatisfactory results in projects and plans previously made.

In 2020's case, mostly, these failures are caused by an epidemic that becomes pandemic and which mundanely ushers-in: **ruin to people's hopes and wishes.**

The other planets involved, only have a minor role to play that only helps or hinders the processes just explained, though with the involvement of planet Jupiter, promises are made, or things made to look promising with this planet's presentation, but can only bring disillusion and disappointment. Jupiter promises much and delivers nothing when the time is right for it to push forward its influence, that is, when it is afflicted by other planets' bad angular relationships to it. Writing this article in April 2020, worry's me because planet Neptune, to some extent, is involved also within the mix, and it [Neptune] may bring, in time, total dissolution, in this case, to the world economies - a sobering thought. Yet, inside this almost Godless society in which we now live, these happenings or events about to happen might be the result of God's intervention; waking us up to where we are as a society on the spiritual plane - which is nowhere! Planet Mercury involved, represents trade and industry, and employment et al, and we may now witness at the time of writing all of this, the Economy is crashing?

****Further: April 5th 2020, the blanket 5G electrical field transmission is being rolled-out whilst we the people have our backs turned the other way because of the government guide-lines as how to protect ourselves against Covid-19 by shutting-down all and everything! I wonder if even the professionals know what Covid-19 really is??????

Is this a conspiracy to stop us protesting against the terrible consequences of drowning us alive with penetratingly powerful microwaves??????

As early as in the 1960's scientists knew, particularly Russian scientists, that those people living near or close to pylons carrying high voltage electrical cables, were at risk health wise - as was proven to be the case.

Imagine what is happening to our body/minds now with radar everywhere, television and radio waves as standard, satellites beaming their rays down on us, and now microwave contamination? Wearing any kind of metal as with jewellery, but especially metal bracelets and necklaces and also metal wrist straps of time-pieces - think again. You are unknowingly drawing to yourself virtually any electrical and magnetic wave that exists?!?! Sit back a moment and think how strange we human-beings are!

What will happen to humanity and other life-forms in time with electrical detrimental fields imposed on us all from below and from above - wires and masts changing and disturbing the **natural** electrical field our bodies possess and enjoy?

All of this is very depressing and very disturbing. Some well known personalities are stating that it is part of a world conspiracy - that may be so, but I personally think it is merely the propagation, the inevitability of those who are passing laws - laws that constrict-us, having mindsets that encourage and praise the need for all people to be vaccinated at any cost, and to take prescribed antibiotics, and other toxic chemico-therapies, and to enjoy the use of micro-wave ovens, and to eat food that is contaminated by insecticides and herbicides, **all as normal.**

Very few of these people are enlightened, and very few have true **vision** as to the bigger picture, as their consciousness is at a basic standard. The basic standard in truth has to be of low-perception consciousness - a manifestation of a blinkered-mind.

This is the limited thinking of most of those beings in charge of us, with a few exceptions. Even so, the logic of these types of mindsets, at their best, will increase peoples' ability to communicate more sophisticatedly, if 5G is made standard, and this will generate good money in the process, as the digital age develops further. The government generating money from major building (bricks & mortar or electronic propagation) projects is perfectly all right in my opinion as long as this money benefits us all - and it usually does in the end (in a democratic system). It is an aspect of the general wealth of the world's largess, especially compared to the state of the world as it was 150 years ago - it's not all bad!

Even so, generally, those who control us, cannot see 'The Bigger Picture' the bigger picture that views the madness that will manifest as a result of this present unnecessary **closing of the economy,** and the **vaccinating** that may be forced on us quite soon, and the rolling-out of **G5** and more.

All of these reduce our immunity to outside pathogens and subsequently the pharmaceutical companies will benefit from the drugs that will ostensibly heal us, **they think**, in their corrupted minds, as we the people suffer various illnesses induced by their wholesale affirmation of harmful influences as stated above, whether by drugs, detrimental electrical/magnetic fields, and toxic food and contaminated water.

Suggesting social distancing and lockdown to the impairment of the Economy, should be a made a criminal offence, especially when implemented as such. Alas, I see only irreparable damage to the people and the Economies of the World. It is not so much the effects of Coved-19, but the terrible effects of the governmental shutdown. It is this total stoppage that is the true virus - a virus that is now accursed because of the wrong dictates taken by governments as they panic without thinking it all through.

WITH ALL THAT HAS JUST BEEN WRITTEN ABOVE, IT WILL SURPRISE PEOPLE WHO MANAGE TO GET TO THE END OF THIS DIATRIBE, THAT THE DETRIMENTAL POSITIONS OF THE PLANETS AT THE TIME OF THE BEGINNING OF THE CHINESE NEW YEAR 2020 WOULD HAVE PRODUCED SOME PROBLEM JUST AS BAD AS THE CURSES THAT WERE/ ARE FOISTED ONTO HUMANITY AS NOW (THIS PANDEMIC), NO MATTER WHAT THE NATURE OF THE PROBLEM WAS/IS - IN OTHER WORDS IF IT HAD NOT BEEN THIS CORROSIVE PANDEMIC COVID-19, IT WOULD HAVE BEEN SOMETHING ELSE JUST AS DESTRUCTIVE - WHO KNOWS: AN INVASION OF ALIENS FROM ANOTHER WORLD WITH THE INTENSION OF THE DESTRUCTION OF HUMANITY?

www.ingramcontent.com/pod-product-compliance
Lightning Source LLC
Chambersburg PA
CBHW080002130626
46553CB00016B/2419